Tales Of The Hall by George Crabbe

George Crabbe was born on December 24th, 1754 in Aldeburgh, Suffolk. He was sent to school at a very young age and soon developed an avid and precocious interest in books.

Crabbe was sent first to a boarding-school at Bungay, and a few years later to a school at Stowmarket, where he learnt mathematics and Latin. His early reading included William Shakespeare, Alexander Pope, Abraham Cowley, Sir Walter Raleigh and Edmund Spenser.

Medicine had now been settled on as his future career and, after three years at Stowmarket, in 1768, he was apprenticed to a local doctor at Wickhambrook, near Bury St Edmunds.

In 1772, a lady's magazine offered a prize for the best poem on 'hope'. Crabbe entered and won. The magazine then printed other short pieces of his during the year.

His first major work, Inebriety, was self-published in 1775. By this time he had completed his medical training and returned to Aldeburgh. Low finances meant his intention to go to London to study at a hospital was abandoned and instead he worked as a warehouseman.

The following year, 1777, he did travel to London to practice medicine, but returned home with financial woes. Crabbe continued to practice as a surgeon but with limited surgical skills, he received only the poorest of patients, together with small and undependable fees.

He moved to London again in April 1780, to see if he could make it as a poet, or, if that failed, as a doctor. By the end of May he had been forced to pawn his surgical instruments.

With the publication in May 1783 of his poem The Village, Crabbe achieved popularity with both the public and critics. Samuel Johnson said of it in a letter to Reynolds "I have sent you back Mr. Crabbe's poem, which I read with great delight. It is original, vigorous, and elegant."

In 1796 their third son, Edmund, died at the age of six. The death shredded Sarah's mental health and she never recovered. Crabbe, a devoted husband, tended her until her death many years later.

In September 1807, Crabbe published a new volume of poems which included The Library, The Newspaper, The Village and The Parish Register, to which were added Sir Eustace Grey and The Hall of Justice. It had been decades since his last publication but now he was seen as an important poet.

Crabbe's next volume of poetry, Tales, was published in 1812. It received a warm welcome from the poet's admirers, and critics. It is now considered Crabbe's masterpiece.

In the summer of 1813, Sarah felt well enough to visit London again. George, Sarah and their two sons spent nearly three months there. The family returned to Muston in September, and at October's end Sarah died at age 63.

In June 1819, Crabbe published his collection Tales of the Hall.

Around 1820 Crabbe began suffering from frequent severe attacks of neuralgia, and this, together with his age, made him less able to travel to London.

In November 1822 he went to see his son George. He was able to preach twice for his son, who congratulated him on the power of his voice. "I will venture a good sum, sir," he said, "that you will be assisting me ten years hence." "Ten weeks" was Crabbe's answer. The prediction proved eerily accurate.

George Crabbe died on February 3rd, 1832, aged 77 at Trowbridge, Wiltshire with his two sons by his side.

Index of Contents

TALES OF THE HALL

TO HER GRACE THE DUCHESS OF RUTLAND

MADAM,

It is the privilege of those who are placed in that elevated situation to which your Grace is an ornament, that they give honour to the person upon whom they confer a favour. When I dedicate to your Grace the fruits of many years, and speak of my debt to the House of Rutland, I feel that I am not without pride in the confession nor insensible to the honour which such gratitude implies. Forty years have elapsed since this debt commenced. On my entrance into the cares of life, and while contending with its difficulties, a Duke and Duchess of Rutland observed and protected me—in my progress a Duke and Duchess of Rutland favoured and assisted me—and, when I am retiring from the world, a Duke and Duchess of Rutland receive my thanks, and accept my offering. All, even in this world of mutability, is not change: I have experienced unvaried favour—I have felt undiminished respect.

With the most grateful remembrance of what I owe, and the most sincere conviction of the little I can return, I present these pages to your Grace's acceptance, and beg leave to subscribe myself,

May it please your Grace,
With respect and gratitude,
Your Grace's
Most obedient and devoted Servant,
GEORGE CRABBE.

Trowbridge,
June, 1819.

PREFACE

If I did not fear that it would appear to my readers like arrogancy, or if it did not seem to myself indecorous to send two volumes of considerable magnitude from the press without preface or apology, without one petition for the reader's attention, or one plea for the writer's defects, I would most willingly spare myself an address of this kind, and more especially for these reasons: first, because a preface is a part of a book seldom honoured by a reader's perusal; secondly, because it is both difficult and distressing to write that which we think will be disregarded; and thirdly, because I do not conceive that I am called upon for such introductory matter by any of the motives which usually influence an author when he composes his prefatory address.

When a writer, whether of poetry or prose, first addresses the public, he has generally something to offer which relates to himself or to his work, and which he considers as a necessary prelude to the work itself, to prepare his readers for the entertainment or the instruction they may expect to receive; for one of these every man who publishes must suppose he affords—this the act itself implies, and in proportion to his conviction of this fact must be his feeling of the difficulty in which he has placed himself: the difficulty consists in reconciling the implied presumption of the undertaking, whether to please or to instruct mankind, with the diffidence and modesty of an untried candidate for fame or favour. Hence originate the many reasons an author assigns for his appearance in that character, whether they actually exist, or are merely offered to hide the motives which cannot be openly avowed: namely, the want or the vanity of the man, as his wishes for profit or reputation may most prevail with him.

Now, reasons of this kind, whatever they may be, cannot be availing beyond their first appearance. An author, it is true, may again feel his former apprehensions, may again be elevated or depressed by the suggestions of vanity and diffidence, and may be again subject to the cold and hot fit of aguish expectation; but he is no more a stranger to the press, nor has the motives or privileges of one who is. With respect to myself, it is certain they belong not to me. Many years have elapsed since I became a candidate for indulgence as an inexperienced writer; and to assume the language of such writer now, and to plead for his indulgences, would be proof of my ignorance of the place assigned to me, and the degree of favour which I have experienced; but of that place I am not uninformed, and with that degree of favour I have no reason to be dissatisfied.

It was the remark of the pious, but on some occasions the querulous, author of the Night Thoughts, that he had "been so long remembered, he was forgotten"—an expression in which there is more appearance of discontent than of submission: if he had patience, it was not the patience that smiles at grief. It is not therefore entirely in the sense of the good Doctor that I apply these words to myself, or to my more early publications. So many years indeed have passed since their first appearance, that I have no reason to complain, on that account, if they be now slumbering with other poems of decent reputation in their day—not dead indeed, nor entirely forgotten, but certainly not the subjects of discussion or conversation as when first introduced to the notice of the public by those whom the public will not forget, whose protection was credit to their author, and whose approbation was fame to them. Still these early publications had so long preceded any other, that, if not altogether unknown, I was, when I came again before the public, in a situation which excused, and perhaps rendered necessary, some explanation; but this also has passed away, and none of my readers will now take the trouble of making any inquiries respecting my motives for writing or for publishing these Tales or verses of any description. Known to each other as readers and authors are known, they will require no preface to bespeak their good will; nor shall I be under the necessity of soliciting the kindness which experience has taught me, endeavouring to merit, I shall not fail to receive.

There is one motive—and it is a powerful one—which sometimes induces an author, and more particularly a poet, to ask the attention of his readers to his prefatory address. This is when he has some favourite and peculiar style or manner which he would explain and defend, and chiefly if he should have adopted a mode of versification of which an uninitiated reader was not likely to perceive either the merit or the beauty. In such case it is natural, and surely pardonable, to assert and to prove, as far as reason will bear us on, that such method of writing has both; to show in what the beauty consists, and what peculiar difficulty there is, which, when conquered, creates the merit. How far any particular poet has or has not succeeded in such attempt is not my business nor my purpose to inquire: I have no peculiar notion to defend, no poetical heterodoxy to support, nor theory of any kind to vindicate or oppose—that which I have used is probably the most common measure in our language; and therefore, whatever be its advantages or defects, they are too well known to require from me a description of the one, or an apology for the other.

Perhaps still more frequent than any explanation of the work is an account of the author himself, the situation in which he is placed, or some circumstances of peculiar kind in his life, education, or employment. How often has youth been pleaded for deficiencies or redundancies, for the existence of which youth may be an excuse, and yet be none for their exposure. Age too has been pleaded for the errors and failings in a work which the octogenarian had the discernment to perceive, and yet had not the fortitude to suppress. Many other circumstances are made apologies for a writer's infirmities: his much employment, and many avocations, adversity, necessity, and the good of mankind. These, or any of them, however availing in themselves, avail not me. I am neither so young nor so old, so much engaged by one pursuit, or by many—I am not so urged by want, or so stimulated by a desire of public benefit—that I can borrow one apology from the many which I have named. How far they prevail with our readers, or with our judges, I cannot tell; and it is unnecessary for me to inquire into the validity of arguments which I have not to produce.

If there be any combination of circumstances which may be supposed to affect the mind of a reader, and in some degree to influence his judgment, the junction of youth, beauty, and merit in a female writer may be allowed to do this; and yet one of the most forbidding of titles is "Poems by a very young Lady"—and this, although beauty and merit were largely insinuated. Ladies, it is true, have of late little need of any indulgence as authors, and names may readily be found which rather excite the envy of man than plead for his lenity. Our estimation of title also in a writer has materially varied from that of our predecessors; "Poems by a Nobleman" would create a very different sensation in our minds from that which was formerly excited when they were so announced. A noble author had then no pretensions to a seat so secure on the "sacred hill," that authors not noble, and critics not gentle, dared not attack; and they delighted to take revenge, by their contempt and derision of the poet, for the pain which their submission and respect to the man had cost them. But in our times we find that a nobleman writes, not merely as well, but better than other men: insomuch that readers in general begin to fancy that the Muses have relinquished their old partiality for rags and a garret, and are become altogether aristocratical in their choice. A conceit so well supported by fact would be readily admitted, did it not appear at the same time, that there were in the higher ranks of society men who could write as tamely, or as absurdly, as they had ever been accused of doing. We may, therefore, regard the works of any noble author as extraordinary productions, but must not found any theory upon them; and, notwithstanding their appearance, must look on genius and talent as we are wont to do on time and chance, that happen indifferently to all mankind.

But, whatever influence any peculiar situation of a writer might have, it cannot be a benefit to me, who have no such peculiarity. I must rely upon the willingness of my readers to be pleased with that which was designed to give them pleasure, and upon the cordiality which naturally springs from a remembrance of our having before parted without any feelings of disgust on the one side, or of mortification on the other.

With this hope I would conclude the present subject; but I am called upon by duty to acknowledge my obligations, and more especially for two of the following Tales—the Story of Lady Barbara, in Book XVI; and that of Ellen in Book XVIII. The first of these I owe to the kindness of a fair friend, who will, I hope, accept the thanks which I very gratefully pay, and pardon me if I have not given to her relation the advantages which she had so much reason to expect. The other story, that of Ellen, could I give it in the language of him who related it to me, would please and affect my readers. It is by no means my only debt, though the one I now more particularly acknowledge; for who shall describe all that he gains in the social, the unrestrained, and the frequent conversations with a friend, who is at once communicative and judicious—whose opinions, on all subjects of literary kind, are founded on good taste, and exquisite feeling? It is one of the greatest "pleasures of my memory" to recal in absence those conversations; and, if I do not in direct terms mention with whom I conversed, it is both because I have no permission, and my readers will have no doubt.

The first intention of the poet must be to please; for, if he means to instruct, he must render the instruction which he hopes to convey palatable and pleasant. I will not assume the tone of a moralist, nor promise that my relations shall be beneficial to mankind; but I have endeavoured, not unsuccessfully I trust, that, in whatsoever I have related or described, there should be nothing introduced which has a tendency to excuse the vices of man by associating with them sentiments that demand our respect, and talents that compel our admiration. There is nothing in these pages which has the mischievous effect of confounding truth and error, or confusing our ideas of right and wrong. I know not which is most injurious to the yielding minds of the young—to render virtue less respectable by making its possessors ridiculous, or by describing vice with so many fascinating qualities, that it is either lost in the assemblage, or pardoned by the association. Man's heart is sufficiently prone to make excuse for man's infirmity, and needs not the aid of poetry, or eloquence, to take from vice its native deformity. A character may be respectable with all its faults, but it must not be made respectable by them. It is grievous when genius will condescend to place strong and evil spirits in a commanding view, or excite our pity and admiration for men of talents, degraded by crime, when struggling with misfortune. It is but too true that great and wicked men may be so presented to us as to demand our applause, when they should excite our abhorrence; but it is surely for the interest of mankind, and our own self-direction, that we should ever keep at unapproachable distance our respect and our reproach.

I have one observation more to offer. It may appear to some that a minister of religion, in the decline of life, should have no leisure for such amusements as these; and for them I have no reply. But to those who are more indulgent to the propensities, the studies, and the habits of mankind, I offer some apology when I produce these volumes, not as the occupations of my life, but the fruits of my leisure— the employment of that time which, if not given to them, had passed in the vacuity of unrecorded idleness, or had been lost in the indulgence of unregistered thoughts and fancies, that melt away in the instant they are conceived, and "leave not a wreck behind."

TALES OF THE HALL

BOOK I

THE HALL

The Meeting of the Brothers, George and Richard—The Retirement of the elder to his native Village— Objects and Persons whom he found there—The Brother described in various Particulars—The Invitation and Journey of the younger—His Soliloquy and Arrival.

TALES OF THE HALL

BOOK I

THE HALL

The Brothers met who many a year had past
Since their last meeting, and that seem'd their last;
They had no parent then or common friend
Who might their hearts to mutual kindness bend;
Who, touching both in their divided state,
Might generous thoughts and warm desires create;
For there are minds whom we must first excite
And urge to feeling, ere they can unite;
As we may hard and stubborn metals beat
And blend together, if we duly heat.
The elder, George, had past his threescore years,
A busy actor, sway'd by hopes and fears
Of powerful kind; and he had fill'd the parts
That try our strength and agitate our hearts.
He married not, and yet he well approved

The social state; but then he rashly loved;
Gave to a strong delusion all his youth,
Led by a vision till alarm'd by truth.
That vision past, and of that truth possest,
His passions wearied and disposed to rest,
George yet had will and power a place to choose,
Where Hope might sleep, and terminate her views.
He chose his native village, and the hill
He climb'd a boy had its attraction still;
With that small brook beneath, where he would stand,
And stooping fill the hollow of his hand,
To quench th' impatient thirst—then stop awhile
To see the sun upon the waters smile,
In that sweet weariness when, long denied,
We drink and view the fountain that supplied
The sparkling bliss—and feel, if not express,
Our perfect ease in that sweet weariness.
The oaks yet flourish'd in that fertile ground,
Where still the church with lofty tower was found;
And still that Hall, a first, a favourite view,
But not the elms that form'd its avenue;
They fell ere George arrived, or yet had stood,
For he in reverence held the living wood,
That widely spreads in earth the deepening root,
And lifts to heaven the still aspiring shoot;
From age to age they fill'd a growing space,
But hid the mansion they were meant to grace.
It was an ancient, venerable hall,
And once surrounded by a moat and wall;
A part was added by a squire of taste,
Who, while unvalued acres ran to waste,
Made spacious rooms, whence he could look about,
And mark improvements as they rose without:
He fill'd the moat, he took the wall away,
He thinn'd the park, and bade the view be gay.
The scene was rich, but he who should behold
Its worth was poor, and so the whole was sold.
Just then our merchant from his desk retired,
And made the purchase that his heart desired—
The Hall of Binning, his delight a boy,
That gave his fancy in her flight employ.
Here, from his father's modest home, he gazed,
Its grandeur charm'd him, and its height amazed,
Work of past ages; and the brick-built place
Where he resided was in much disgrace;
But never in his fancy's proudest dream
Did he the master of that mansion seem.
Young was he then, and little did he know

What years on care and diligence bestow;
Now, young no more, retired to views well known,
He finds that object of his awe his own:
The Hall at Binning!—how he loves the gloom
That sun-excluding window gives the room;
Those broad brown stairs on which he loves to tread;
Those beams within; without, that length of lead,
On which the names of wanton boys appear,
Who died old men, and left memorials here—
Carvings of feet and hands, and knots and flowers,
The fruits of busy minds in idle hours.
Here, while our squire the modern part possess'd,
His partial eye upon the old would rest;
That best his comforts gave—this sooth'd his feelings best.
Here, day by day, withdrawn from busy life,
No child t' awake him, to engage no wife,
When friends were absent, not to books inclined,
He found a sadness steal upon his mind;
Sighing the works of former lords to see,
"I follow them," he cried, "but who will follow me?"
Some ancient men whom he a boy had known
He knew again; their changes were his own.
Comparing now he view'd them, and he felt
That time with him in lenient mood had dealt;
While some the half-distinguish'd features bore
That he was doubtful if he saw before,
And some in memory lived, whom he must see no more.
Here George had found, yet scarcely hoped to find,
Companions meet, minds fitted to his mind;
Here, late and loth, the worthy rector came,
From college dinners and a fellow's fame;
Yet, here when fix'd, was happy to behold
So near a neighbour in a friend so old.
Boys on one form they parted, now to meet
In equal state, their worships on one seat.
Here were a sister-pair, who seem'd to live
With more respect than affluence can give;
Although not affluent, they, by nature graced,
Had sense and virtue, dignity and taste;
Their minds by sorrows, by misfortunes tried,
Were vex'd and heal'd, were pain'd and purified.
Hither a sage physician came, and plann'd,
With books his guides, improvements on his land;
Nor less to mind than matter would he give
His noble thoughts, to know how spirits live,
And what is spirit; him his friends advised
To think with fear; but caution he despised;
And hints of fear provoked him till he dared

Beyond himself, nor bold assertion spared,
But fiercely spoke, like those who strongly feel,
"Priests and their craft, enthusiasts and their zeal.'
More yet appear'd, of whom as we proceed—
Ah! y eld not yet to languor—you shall read.
But ere the events that from this meeting rose,
Be they of pain or pleasure, we disclose,
It is of custom, doubtless is of use,
That we our heroes first should introduce.
Come, then, fair Truth! and let me clearly see
The minds I paint, as they are seen in thee;
To me their merits and their faults impart;
Give me to say, "frail being! such thou art,"
And closely let me view the naked human heart.
GEORGE loved to think; but, as he late began
To muse on all the grander thoughts of man,
He took a solemn and a serious view
Of his religion, and he found it true;
Firmly, yet meekly, he his mind applied
To this great subject, and was satisfied.
He then proceeded, not so much intent,
But st ll in earnest, and to church he went.
Although they found some difference in their creed,
He and his pastor cordially agreed,
Convinced that they who would the truth obtain
By disputation, find their efforts vain;
The church he view'd as liberal minds will view,
And there he fix'd his principles and pew.
He saw—he thought he saw—how weakness, pride,
And habit, draw seceding crowds aside:
Weakness, that loves on trifling points to dwell;
Pride, that at first from Heaven's own worship fell;
And habit, going where it went before,
Or to the meeting or the tavern door.
George loved the cause of freedom, but reproved
All who with wild and boyish ardour loved:
Those who believed they never could be free,
Except when fighting for their liberty;
Who by their very clamour and complaint
Invite coercion or enforce restraint.
He thought a trust so great, so good a cause,
Was only to be kept by guarding laws;
For, public blessings firmly to secure,
We must a lessening of the good endure.
The public waters are to none denied;
All drink the stream, but only few must guide.
There must be reservoirs to hold supply,
And channels form'd to send the blessing by;

The public good must be a private care;
None all they would may have, but all a share.
So we must freedom with restraint enjoy;
What crowds possess they will, uncheck'd, destroy;
And hence, that freedom may to all be dealt,
Guards must be fix'd, and safety must be felt.
So thought our squire, nor wish'd the guards t' appear
So strong, that safety might be bought too dear;
The constitution was the ark that he
Join'd to support with zeal and sanctity;
Nor would expose it, as th' accursed son
His father's weakness, to be gazed upon.
"I for that freedom make," said he, "my prayer,
That suits with all, like atmospheric air;
That is to mortal man by heaven assign'd,
Who cannot bear a pure and perfect kind.
The lighter gas, that, taken in the frame,
The spirit heats, and sets the blood in flame:
Such is the freedom which when men approve,
They know not what a dangerous thing they love."
George chose the company of men of sense,
But could with wit in moderate share dispense;
He wish'd in social ease his friends to meet,
When still he thought the female accent sweet;
Well from the ancient, better from the young,
He loved the lispings of the mother tongue.
He ate and drank, as much as men who think
Of life's best pleasures, ought to eat or drink;
Men purely temperate might have taken less,
But still he loved indulgence, not excess;
Nor would alone the grants of fortune taste,
But shared the wealth he judged it crime to waste;
And thus obtained the sure reward of care—
For none can spend like him who learns to spare.
Time, thought, and trouble made the man appear—
By nature shrewd—sarcastic and severe;
Still, he was one whom those who fully knew
Esteem'd and trusted, one correct and true;
All on his word with surety might depend,
Kind as a man, and faithful as a friend.
But him the many [knew] not, knew not cause
In their new squire for censure or applause;
Ask them, "Who dwelt within that lofty wall?"
And they would say, "the gentleman was tall;
Look'd old when follow'd, but alert when met,
And had some vigour in his movements yet;
He stoops, but not as one infirm; and wears
Dress that becomes his station and his years."

Such was the man who from the world return'd
Nor friend nor foe; he prized it not, nor spurn'd;
But came and sat him in his village down,
Safe from its smile, and careless of its frown:
He, fairly looking into life's account,
Saw frowns and favours were of like amount;
And viewing all—his perils, prospects, purse—
He said, "Content! 'tis well it is no worse."
Through ways more rough had fortune RICHARD led,
The world he traversed was the book he read;
Hence clashing notions and opinions strange
Lodged in his mind: all liable to change.
By nature generous, open, daring, free,
The vce he hated was hypocrisy.
Religious notions, in her latter years,
His mother gave, admonish'd by her fears;
To these he added, as he chanced to read
A pious work or learn a christian creed.
He heard the preacher by the highway side,
The church's teacher, and the meeting's guide;
And, mixing all their matters in his brain,
Distill'd a something he could ill explain;
But still it served him for his daily use,
And kept his lively passions from abuse;
For he believed, and held in reverence high,
The truth so dear to man—"not all shall die."
The minor portions of his creed hung loose,
For time to shapen and an whole produce;
This love effected, and a favourite maid
With clearer views his honest flame repaid;
Hers was the thought correct, the hope sublime,
She shaped his creed, and did the work of time.
He spake of freedom as a nation's cause,
And loved, like George, our liberty and laws;
But had more youthful ardour to be free,
And stronger fears for injured liberty.
With him, on various questions that arose,
The monarch's servants were the people's foes;
And, though he fought with all a Briton's zeal,
He felt for France as Freedom's children feel;
Went far with her in what she thought reform,
And hail'd the revolutionary storm;
Yet would not here, where there was least to win,
And most to lose, the doubtful work begin;
But look'd on change with some religious fear,
And cried, with filial dread, "Ah! come not here."
His friends he did not as the thoughtful choose;
Long to deliberate was, he judged, to lose;

Frankly he join'd the free, nor suffered pride
Or doubt to part them, whom their fate allied;
Men with such minds at once each other aid;
"Frankness," they cry, "with frankness is repaid;
If honest, why suspect? if poor, of what afraid?
Wealth's timid votaries may with caution move;
Be it our wisdom to confide and love."
So pleasures came, (not purchased first or plann'd)
But the chance pleasures that the poor command;
They came but seldom, they remain'd not long,
Nor gave him time to question "are they wrong?"
These he enjoy'd, and left to after time
To judge the folly or decide the crime;
Sure had he been, he had perhaps been pure
From this reproach—but Richard was not sure—
Yet from the sordid vice, the mean, the base,
He stood aloof—death frown'd not like disgrace.
With handsome figure, and with manly air,
He pleased the sex, who all to him were fair;
With filial love he look'd on forms decay'd,
And admiration's debt to beauty paid;
On sea or land, wherever Richard went,
He felt affection, and he found content;
There was in him a strong presiding hope
In fortune's tempests, and it bore him up.
But when that mystic vine his mansion graced,
When numerous branches round his board were placed,
When sighs of apprehensive love were heard—
Then first the spirit of the hero fear'd;
Then he reflected on the father's part,
And all an husband's sorrow touch'd his heart;
Then thought he, "Who will their assistance lend?
And be the children's guide, the parent's friend?
Who shall their guardian, their protector be?
I have a brother—Well!—and so has he."
And now they met; a message—kind, 'tis true,
But verbal only—ask'd an interview;
And many a mile, perplex'd by doubt and fear,
Had Richard past, unwilling to appear—
"How shall I now my unknown way explore,
He proud and rich—I very proud and poor?
Perhaps my friend a dubious speech mistook,
And George may meet me with a stranger's look
Then to my home when I return again,
How shall I bear this business to explain,
And tell of hopes raised high, and feelings hurt, in vain?
"How stands the case? My brother's friend and mine
Met at an inn, and sat them down to dine:

When, having settled all their own affairs,
And kindly canvass'd such as were not theirs,
Just as my friend was going to retire—
'Stay!—you will see the brother of our squire,'
Said h s companion; 'be his friend, and tell
The captain that his brother loves him well,
And, when he has no better thing in view,
Will be rejoiced to see him. Now, adieu!'
Well! here I am; and, brother, take you heed,
I am not come to flatter you and feed;
You shall no soother, fawner, hearer find,
I will not brush your coat, nor smooth your mind;
I will not hear your tales the whole day long,
Nor swear you're right if I believe you wrong.
Nor be a witness of the facts you state,
Nor as my own adopt your love or hate:
I will not earn my dinner when I dine,
By taking all your sentiments for mine;
Nor watch the guiding motions of your eye,
Before I venture question or reply;
Nor when you speak affect an awe profound,
Sinking my voice, as if I fear'd the sound;
Nor to your looks obediently attend,
The poor, the humble, the dependant friend;
Yet, son of that dear mother could I meet—
But lo! the mansion—'tis a fine old seat!"
The Brothers met, with both too much at heart
To be observant of each other's part.
"Brother, I'm glad," was all that George could say,
Then stretch'd his hand, and turn'd his head away;
For he in tender tears had no delight,
But scorn'd the thought, and ridiculed the sight;
Yet now with pleasure, though with some surprise,
He felt his heart o'erflowing at his eyes.
Richard, mean time, made some attempts to speak,
Strong in his purpose, in his trial weak;
We cannot nature by our wishes rule,
Nor at our will her warm emotions cool;—
At length affection, like a risen tide,
Stood still, and then seem'd slowly to subside;
Each on the other's looks had power to dwell,
And Brother Brother greeted passing well.

Further Account of the Meeting—Of the Men—The Mother—The Uncle—The private Tutor—The second Husband—Dinner Conversation— School of the Rector and Squire—The Master.

TALES OF THE HALL

BOOK II

THE BROTHERS

At length the Brothers met, no longer tried
By those strong feelings that in time subside;
Not fluent yet their language, but the eye
And action spoke both question and reply;
Till the heart rested, and could calmly feel;
Till the shook compass felt the settling steel;
Till playful smiles on graver converse broke,
And either speaker less abruptly spoke.
Still was there oft-times silence, silence blest,
Expressive, thoughtful—their emotions' rest:
Pauses that came not from a want of thought,
But want of ease, by wearied passion sought;
For souls, when hurried by such powerful force,
Rest, and retrace the pleasure of the course.
They differ'd much; yet might observers trace
Likeness of features both in mind and face;
Pride they possess'd, that neither strove to hide,
But not offensive, not obtrusive pride.
Unlike had been their life, unlike the fruits
Of different tempers, studies, and pursuits;
Nay, in such varying scenes the men had moved,
'Twas passing strange that aught alike they loved.
But all distinction now was thrown apart,
While these strong feelings ruled in either heart.
As various colours in a painted ball,
While it has rest, are seen distinctly all,
Till, whirl'd around by some exterior force,
They all are blended in the rapid course:
So in repose, and not by passion sway'd,
We saw the difference by their habits made;
But, tried by strong emotions, they became
Fill'd with one love, and were in heart the same;

Joy to the face its own expression sent,
And gave a likeness in the looks it lent.
All now was sober certainty; the joy
That no strong passions swell till they destroy:
For they, like wine, our pleasures raise so high,
That they subdue our strength, and then they die.
George in his brother felt a glowing pride,
He wonder'd who that fertile mind supplied—
"Where could the wanderer gather on his road
Knowledge so various? how the mind this food?
No college train'd him, guideless through his life,
Without a friend—not so! he has a wife.
Ah! had I married, I might now have seen
My—No! it never, never could have been,
That long enchantment, that pernicious state!—
True, I recover'd, but alas! too late—
And here is Richard, poor indeed—but—nay!
This is self-torment—foolish thoughts, away!"
Ease leads to habit, as success to ease,
He lives by rule who lives himself to please;
For change is trouble, and a man of wealth
Consults his quiet as he guards his health;
And habit now on George had sovereign power,
His actions all had their accustom'd hour:
At the fix'd time he slept, he walk'd, he read,
Or sought his grounds, his gruel, and his bed;
For every season he with caution dress'd,
And morn and eve had the appropriate vest;
He talk'd of early mists, and night's cold air,
And in one spot was fix'd his worship's chair.
But not a custom yet on Richard's mind
Had force, or him to certain modes confined;
To him no joy such frequent visits paid
That habit by its beaten track was made;
He was not one who at his ease could say,
"We'll live to-morrow as we lived to-day;"
But he and his were as the ravens fed,
As the day came it brought the daily bread.
George, born to fortune, though of moderate kind,
Was not in haste his road through life to find.
His father early lost, his mother tried
To live without him, liked it not, and—sigh'd,
When, for her widow'd hand, an amorous youth applied.
She still was young, and felt that she could share
A lover's passion, and an husband's care;
Yet past twelve years before her son was told,
To his surprise, "your father you behold."
But he beheld not with his mother's eye

The new relation, and would not comply,
But all obedience, all connexion spurn'd,
And fled their home, where he no more return'd.
His father's brother was a man whose mind
Was to his business and his bank confined;
His guardian care the captious nephew sought,
And was received, caress'd, advised, and taught.
"That Irish beggar, whom your mother took,
Does you this good, he sends you to your book;
Yet love not books beyond their proper worth,
But, when they fit you for the world, go forth:
They are like beauties, and may blessings prove,
When we with caution study them, or love;
But, when to either we our souls devote,
We grow unfitted for that world, and dote."
George to a school of higher class was sent,
But he was ever grieving that he went:
A still, retiring, musing, dreaming boy,
He relish'd not their sudden bursts of joy;
Nor the tumultuous pleasures of a rude,
A noisy, careless, fearless multitude.
He had his own delights, as one who flies
From every pleasure that a crowd supplies;
Thrice he return'd, but then was weary grown,
And was indulged with studies of his own.
Still could the rector and his friend relate
The small adventures of that distant date;
And Richard listen'd as they spake of time
Past in that world of misery and crime.
Freed from his school, a priest of gentle kind
The uncle found to guide the nephew's mind;
Pleased with his teacher, George so long remain'd,
The mind was weaken'd by the store it gain'd.
His guardian uncle, then on foreign ground,
No time to think of his improvements found;
Nor had the nephew, now to manhood grown,
Talents or taste for trade or commerce shown,
But shunn'd a world of which he little knew,
Nor of that little did he like the view.
His mother chose, nor I the choice upbraid,
An Irish soldier of an house decay'd,
And passing poor; but, precious in her eyes
As she in his, they both obtain'd a prize.
To do the captain justice, she might share
What of her jointure his affairs could spare;
Irish he was in his profusion—true,
But he was Irish in affection too;
And, though he spent her wealth and made her grieve,

He always said "my dear" and "with your leave."
Him she survived; she saw his boy possess'd
Of manly spirit, and then sank to rest.
Her sons thus left, some legal cause required
That they should meet, but neither this desired.
George, a recluse, with mind engaged, was one
Who did no business, with whom none was done;
Whose heart, engross'd by its peculiar care,
Shared no one's counsel—no one his might share.
Richard, a boy, a lively boy, was told
Of his half-brother, haughty, stern, and cold;
And his boy folly, or his manly pride,
Made him on measures cool and harsh decide.
So, when they met, a distant cold salute
Was of a long-expected day the fruit;
The rest by proxies managed, each withdrew,
Vex'd by the business and the brother too;
But now they met when time had calm'd the mind,
Both wish'd for kindness, and it made them kind.
George had no wife or child, and was disposed
To love the man on whom his hope reposed:
Richard had both; and those so well beloved,
Husband and father were to kindness moved;
And thus th' affections check'd, subdued, restrain'd
Rose in their force, and in their fulness reign'd.
The bell now bids to dine; the friendly priest,
Social and shrewd, the day's delight increased.
Brief and abrupt their speeches while they dined,
Nor were their themes of intellectual kind;
Nor, dinner past, did they to these advance,
But left the subjects they discuss'd to chance.
Richard, whose boyhood in the place was spent,
Profound attention to the speakers lent,
Who spake of men; and, as he heard a name,
Actors and actions to his memory came.
Then, too, the scenes he could distinctly trace,
Here he had fought, and there had gain'd a race;
In that church-walk he had affrighted been;
In that old tower he had a something seen—
What time, dismiss'd from school, he upward cast
A fearful look, and trembled as he past.
No private tutor Richard's parents sought,
Made keen by hardship, and by trouble taught;
They might have sent him—some the counsel gave—
Seven gloomy winters of the North to brave:
Where a few pounds would pay for board and bed,
While the poor frozen boy was taught and fed;
When, say he lives, fair, freckled, lank and lean,

The lad returns shrewd, subtle, close and keen;
With all the northern virtues, and the rules
Taught to the thrifty in these thriving schools.
There had he gone, and borne this trying part—
But Richard's mother had a mother's heart.
Now squire and rector were return'd to school,
And spoke of him who there had sovereign rule:
He was, it seem'd, a tyrant of the sort
Who make the cries of tortured boys his sport;
One of a race, if not extinguish'd, tamed—
The flogger now is of the act ashamed;
But this great mind all mercy's calls withstood;
This Holofernes was a man of blood.
"Students," he said, "like horses on the road,
Must well be lash'd before they take the load;
They may be willing for a time to run,
But you must whip them ere the work be done.
To tell a boy, that, if he will improve,
His friends will praise him, and his parents love,
Is doing nothing—he has not a doubt
But they will love him, nay, applaud, without;
Let no fond sire a boy's ambition trust,
To make him study, let him see he must."
Such his opinion; and, to prove it true,
At least sincere, it was his practice too.
Pluto they call'd him, and they named him well:
'Twas not an heaven where he was pleased to dwell.
From him a smile was like the Greenland sun,
Surprising, nay portentous, when it shone;
Or like the lightning, for the sudden flash
Prepared the children for the thunder's crash.
O! had Narcissa, when she fondly kiss'd
The weeping boy whom she to school dismiss'd,
Had she beheld him shrinking from the arm
Uplifted high to do the greater harm,
Then seen her darling stript, and that pure white,
And—O! her soul had fainted at the sight;
And with those looks that love could not withstand,
She would have cried, "Barbarian, hold thy hand!"
In vain! no grief to this stern soul could speak,
No iron-tear roll down this Pluto's cheek.
Thus far they went, half earnest, half in jest,
Then turn'd to themes of deeper interest;
While Richard's mind, that for awhile had stray'd,
Call'd home its powers, and due attention paid.

BOOK III

BOYS AT SCHOOL

The School—School-Boys—The Boy-Tyrant—Sir Hector Blane— School-Boys in after Life, how changed— how the same—The patronized Boy, his Life and Death—Reflections—Story of Harry Bland.

TALES OF THE HALL

BOOK III

BOYS AT SCHOOL

We name the world a school, for day by day
We something learn, till we are call'd away;
The school we name a world,—for vice and pain,
Fraud and contention, there begin to reign;
And much, in fact, this lesser world can show
Of grief and crime that in the greater grow.
"You saw," said George, "in that still-hated school
How the meek suffer, how the haughty rule;
There soft, ingenuous, gentle minds endure
Ills that ease, time, and friendship fail to cure;
There the best hearts, and those, who shrink from sin,
Find some seducing imp to draw them in,
Who takes infernal pleasure to impart
The strongest poison to the purest heart.
Call to your mind this scene—Yon boy behold:
How hot the vengeance of a heart so cold!
See how he beats, whom he had just reviled
And made rebellious—that imploring child;
How fierce his eye, how merciless his blows,
And how his anger on his insult grows;
You saw this Hector and his patient slave,
Th' insulting speech, the cruel blows he gave.
Mix'd with mankind, his interest in his sight,
We found this Nimrod civil and polite;
There was no triumph in his manner seen,
He was so humble you might think him mean.
Those angry passions slept till he attain'd
His purposed wealth, and waked when that was gain'd;
He then resumed the native wrath and pride,
The more indulged, as longer laid aside;

Wife, children, servants, all obedience pay,
The slaves at school no greater slaves than they;
No more dependant, he resumes the rein,
And shows the school-boy turbulence again.
"Were I a poet, I would say, he brings
To recollection some impetuous springs;
See one that issues from its humble source,
To gain new powers, and run its noisy course:
Frothy and fierce among the rocks it goes,
And threatens all that bound it or oppose;
Till wider grown, and finding large increase,
Though bounded still, it moves along in peace;
And, as its waters to the ocean glide,
They bear a busy people on its tide;
But there arrived, and from its channel free,
Those swelling waters meet the mighty sea;
With threat'ning force the new-form'd billows swell,
And now affright the crowd they bore so well."
"Yet," said the rector, "all these early signs
Of vice are lost, and vice itself declines;
Religion counsels; troubles, sorrows rise,
And the vile spirit in the conflict dies.
"Sir Hector Blane, the champion of the school,
Was very blockhead, but was form'd for rule;
Learn he could not; he said he could not learn,
But he profess'd it gave him no concern.
Books were his horror, dinner his delight,
And his amusement to shake hands and fight;
Argue he could not, but in case of doubt,
Or disputation, fairly box'd it out.
This was his logic, and his arm so strong,
His cause prevail'd, and he was never wrong;
But so obtuse—you must have seen his look,
Desponding, angry, puzzled o'er his book.
"Can you not see him on the morn that proved
His skill in figures? Pluto's self was moved—
'Come, six times five?' th' impatient teacher cried;
In vain, the pupil shut his eyes, and sigh'd.
'Try, six times count your fingers; how he stands!—
Your fingers, idiot!'—'What, of both my hands?'
"With parts like these his father felt assured,
In busy times, a ship might be procured;
He too was pleased to be so early freed:
He now could fight, and he in time might read.
So he has fought, and in his country's cause
Has gain'd him glory, and our hearts' applause.
No more the blustering boy a school defies;
We see the hero from the tyrant rise,

And in the captain's worth the student's dulness dies."
"Be all allow'd;" replied the squire, "I give
Praise to his actions; may their glory live!
Nay, I will hear him in his riper age
Fight his good ship, and with the foe engage;
Nor will I quit him when the cowards fly,
Although, like them, I dread his energy.
"But still, my friend, that ancient spirit reigns;
His powers support the credit of his brains,
Insisting ever that he must be right,
And for his reasons still prepared to fight.
Let him a judge of England's prowess be,
And all her floating terrors on the sea;
But this contents not, this is not denied;
He claims a right on all things to decide,
A kind of patent-wisdom; and he cries,
''Tis so!' and bold the hero that denies.
Thus the boy-spirit still the bosom rules,
And the world's maxims were at first the school's."
"No doubt," said Jacques, "there are in minds the seeds
Of good and ill, the virtues and the weeds;
But is it not of study the intent
This growth of evil nature to prevent?
To check the progress of each idle shoot
That might retard the ripening of the fruit?
Our purpose certain, and we much effect,
We something cure, and something we correct;
But do your utmost: when the man you see,
You find him what you saw the boy would be,
Disguised a little; but we still behold
What pleased and what offended us of old.
Years from the mind no native stain remove,
But lay the varnish of the world above.
Still, when he can, he loves to step aside
And be the boy, without a check or guide;
In the old wanderings he with pleasure strays,
And reassumes the bliss of earlier days.
"I left at school the boy with pensive look,
Whom some great patron order'd to his book;
Who from his mother's cot reluctant came,
And gave my lord, for this compassion, fame;
Who, told of all his patron's merit, sigh'd,
I know not why, in sorrow or in pride;
And would, with vex'd and troubled spirit, cry,
'I am not happy; let your envy die.'
Him left I with you; who, perhaps, can tell
If fortune bless'd him, or what fate befell.
I yet remember how the idlers ran

To see the carriage of the godlike man,
When pride restrain'd me; yet I thought the deed
Was noble, too—and how did it succeed?"
Jacques answer'd not till he had backward cast
His view, and dwelt upon the evil past;
Then, as he sigh'd, he smil'd;—from folly rise
Such smiles, and misery will create such sighs.
And Richard now from his abstraction broke,
Listening attentive as the rector spoke.

"This noble lord was one disposed to try
And weigh the worth of each new luxury;
Now, at a certain time, in pleasant mood,
He tried the luxury of doing good.
For this he chose a widow's handsome boy,
Whom he would first improve, and then employ.
The boy was gentle, modest, civil, kind,
But not for bustling through the world design'd;
Reserved in manner, with a little gloom,
Apt to retire, but never to assume;
Possess'd of pride that he could not subdue,
Although he kept his origin in view.
Him sent my lord to school, and this became
A theme for praise, and gave his lordship fame;
But when the boy was told how great his debt,
He proudly ask'd, 'is it contracted yet?'
"With care he studied, and with some success;
His patience great, but his acquirements less:
Yet when he heard that Charles would not excel,
His lordship answer'd, with a smile, ''tis well;
Let him proceed, and do the best he can,
I want no pedant, but a useful man.'
"The speech was heard, and praise was amply dealt,
His lordship felt it, and he said he felt—
'It is delightful,' he observed, 'to raise
And foster merit—it is more than praise.'
"Five years at school th' industrious boy had past,
'And what,' was whisper'd, 'will be done at last?'
"My lord was troubled, for he did not mean
To have his bounty watch'd and overseen;
Bounty that sleeps when men applaud no more
The generous act that waked their praise before;
The deed was pleasant while the praise was new,
But none the progress would with wonder view.
It was a debt contracted; he who pays
A debt is just, but must not look for praise:
The deed that once had fame must still proceed,
Though fame no more proclaims 'how great the deed!'

The boy is taken from his mother's side,
And he who took him must be now his guide.
But this, alas! instead of bringing fame,
A tax, a trouble, to my lord became.
"'The boy is dull, you say,—why then by trade,
By law, by physic, nothing can be made;
If a small living—mine are both too large,
And then the college is a cursed charge.
The sea is open; should he there display
Signs of dislike, he cannot run away.'
"Now Charles, who acted no heroic part,
And felt no seaman's glory warm his heart,
Refused the offer—anger touch'd my lord.—
'He does not like it—Good, upon my word—
If I at college place him, he will need
Supplies for ever, and will not succeed;—
Doubtless in me 'tis duty to provide
Not for his comfort only, but his pride—
Let him to sea!'—He heard the words again,
With promise join'd—with threat'ning; all in vain:
Charles had his own pursuits; for aid to these
He had been thankful, and had tried to please;
But urged again, as meekly as a saint,
He humbly begg'd to stay at home, and paint.
'Yes, pay some dauber, that this stubborn fool
May grind his colours, and may boast his school.'
"As both persisted, 'Choose, good sir, your way,'
The peer exclaim'd, 'I have no more to say,
I seek your good, but I have no command
Upon your will, nor your desire withstand.'
"Resolved and firm, yet dreading to offend,
Charles pleaded genius with his noble friend:
'Genius!' he cried, 'the name that triflers give
To their strong wishes without pains to live;
Genius! the plea of all who feel desire
Of fame, yet grudge the labours that acquire—
But say 'tis true: how poor, how late the gain,
And certain ruin if the hope be vain!'
Then to the world appeal'd my lord, and cried,
'Whatever happens, I am justified.'
Nay, it was trouble to his soul to find
There was such hardness in the human mind:
He wash'd his hands before the world, and swore
That he 'such minds would patronize no more.'
"Now Charles his bread by daily labours sought,
And this his solace, 'so Corregio wrought.'
Alas, poor youth! however great his name,
And humble thine, thy fortune was the same.

Charles drew and painted, and some praise obtain'd
For care and pains; but little more was gain'd:
Fame was his hope, and he contempt display'd
For approbation, when 'twas coolly paid;
His daily tasks he call'd a waste of mind,
Vex'd at his fate, and angry with mankind:
'Thus have the blind to merit ever done,
And Genius mourn'd for each neglected son.'
"Charles murmur'd thus, and, angry and alone,
Half breathed the curse, and half suppress'd the groan;
Then still more sullen grew, and still more proud;
Fame so refused he to himself allow'd;
Crowds in contempt he held, and all to him was crowd.
"If aught on earth, the youth his mother loved,
And, at her death, to distant scenes removed.
"Years past away, and where he lived, and how,
Was then unknown—indeed we know not now;
But once at twilight walking up and down,
In a poor alley of the mighty town,
Where, in her narrow courts and garrets, hide
The grieving sons of genius, want, and pride,
I met him musing; sadness I could trace,
And conquer'd hope's meek anguish, in his face.
See him I must; but I with ease address'd,
And neither pity nor surprise express'd;
I strove both grief and pleasure to restrain,
But yet I saw that I was giving pain.
He said, with quick'ning pace, as loth to hold
A longer converse, that 'the day was cold,
That he was well, that I had scarcely light
To aid my steps,' and bade me then good night!
"I saw him next where he had lately come,
A silent pauper in a crowded room;
I heard his name, but he conceal'd his face,
To his sad mind his misery was disgrace;
In vain I strove to combat his disdain
Of my compassion—'Sir, I pray, refrain;'
For I had left my friends and stepp'd aside,
Because I fear'd his unrelenting pride.
"He then was sitting on a workhouse-bed,
And on the naked boards reclined his head,
Around were children with incessant cry,
And near was one, like him, about to die;
A broken chair's deal bottom held the store
That he required—he soon would need no more;
A yellow tea-pot, standing at his side,
From its half-spout the cold, black tea supplied.
"Hither, it seem'd, the fainting man was brought,

Found without food—it was no longer sought;
For his employers knew not whom they paid,
Nor where to seek him whom they wish'd to aid.
Here brought, some kind attendant he address'd,
And sought some trifles which he yet possess'd;
Then named a lightless closet, in a room
Hired at small rate, a garret's deepest gloom.
They sought the region, and they brought him all
That he his own, his proper wealth could call:
A better coat, less pieced; some linen neat,
Not whole; and papers, many a valued sheet—
Designs and drawings; these, at his desire,
Were placed before him at the chamber fire,
And while th' admiring people stood to gaze,
He, one by one, committed to the blaze,
Smiling in spleen; but one he held awhile,
And gave it to the flames, and could not smile.
"The sickening man—for such appear'd the fact—
Just in his need, would not a debt contract;
But left his poor apartment for the bed
That earth might yield him, or some way-side shed;
Here he was found, and to this place convey'd,
Where he might rest, and his last debt be paid:
Fame was his wish, but he so far from fame,
That no one knew his kindred, or his name,
Or by what means he lived, or from what place he came.
"Poor Charles! unnoticed by thy titled friend,
Thy days had calmly past, in peace thine end;
Led by thy patron's vanity astray,
Thy own misled thee in thy trackless way,
Urging thee on by hope absurd and vain,
Where never peace or comfort smiled again!
"Once more I saw him, when his spirits fail'd,
And my desire to aid him then prevail'd;
He show'd a softer feeling in his eye,
And watch'd my looks, and own'd the sympathy.
'Twas now the calm of wearied pride; so long
As he had strength was his resentment strong;
But in such place, with strangers all around,
And they such strangers, to have something found
Allied to his own heart, an early friend—
One, only one, who would on him attend,
To give and take a look at this his journey's end!
One link, however slender, of the chain
That held him where he could not long remain;
The one sole interest!—No, he could not now
Retain his anger; Nature knew not how;
And so there came a softness to his mind,

And he forgave the usage of mankind.
His cold long fingers now were press'd to mine,
And his faint smile of kinder thoughts gave sign;
His lips moved often as he tried to lend
His words their sound, and softly whisper'd 'friend!'
Not without comfort in the thought express'd
By that calm look with which he sank to rest."

"The man," said George, "you see, through life retain'd
The boy's defects; his virtues too remain'd.
"But where are now those minds so light and gay,
So forced on study, so intent on play,
Swept, by the world's rude blasts, from hope's dear views away
Some grieved for long neglect in earlier times,
Some sad from frailties, some lamenting crimes;
Thinking, with sorrow, on the season lent
For noble purpose, and in trifling spent;
And now, at last, when they in earnest view
The nothings done—what work they find to do!
Where is that virtue that the generous boy
Felt, and resolved that nothing should destroy?
He who with noble indignation glow'd
When vice had triumph? who his tear bestow'd
On injured merit? he who would possess
Power, but to aid the children of distress;
Who has such joy in generous actions shown,
And so sincere, they might be call'd his own;
Knight, hero, patriot, martyr! on whose tongue,
And potent arm, a nation's welfare hung;
He who to public misery brought relief,
And soothed the anguish of domestic grief?
Where now this virtue's fervour, spirit, zeal?
Who felt so warmly, has he ceased to feel?
The boy's emotions of that noble kind,
Ah! sure th' experienced man has not resign'd;
Or are these feelings varied? has the knight,
Virtue's own champion, now refused to fight?
Is the deliverer turn'd th' oppressor now?
Has the reformer dropt the dangerous vow?
Or has the patriot's bosom lost its heat,
And forced him, shivering, to a snug retreat?
Is such the grievous lapse of human pride?
Is such the victory of the worth untried?
"Here will I pause, and then review the shame
Of Harry Bland, to hear his parent's name.
That mild, that modest boy, whom well we knew,
In him long time the secret sorrow grew;
He wept alone; then to his friend confess'd

The grievous fears that his pure mind oppress'd;
And thus, when terror o'er his shame obtain'd
A painful conquest, he his case explain'd;
And first his favourite question'd—'Willie, tell,
Do all the wicked people go to hell?'
"Willie with caution answer'd, 'Yes, they do,
Or else repent; but what is this to you?'
'O! yes, dear friend:' he then his tale began—
'He fear'd his father was a wicked man,
Nor had repented of his naughty life;
The w fe he had indeed was not a wife,
Not as my mother was; the servants all
Call her a name—I'll whisper what they call.
She saw me weep, and ask'd, in high disdain,
If tears could bring my mother back again?
This I could bear, but not when she pretends
Such fond regard, and what I speak commends;
Talks of my learning, fawning wretch! and tries
To make me love her,—love! when I despise.
Indeed I had it in my heart to say
Words of reproach, before I came away;
And then my father's look is not the same,
He puts his anger on to hide his shame.'
"With all these feelings delicate and nice,
This dread of infamy, this scorn of vice,
He left the school, accepting, though with pride,
His father's aid—but there would not reside;
He married then a lovely maid, approved
Of every heart as worthy to be loved;
Mild as the morn in summer, firm as truth,
And graced with wisdom in the bloom of youth.
"How is it, men, when they in judgment sit
On the same fault, now censure, now acquit?
Is it not thus, that here we view the sin,
And there the powerful cause that drew us in?
'Tis not that men are to the evil blind,
But that a different object fills the mind.
In judging others we can see too well
Their grievous fall, but not how grieved they fell;
Judging ourselves, we to our minds recall,
Not how we fell, but how we grieved to fall.
Or could this man, so vex'd in early time,
By this strong feeling for his father's crime;
Who to the parent's sin was barely just,
And mix'd with filial fear the man's disgust—
Could he, without some strong delusion, quit
The path of duty, and to shame submit?
Cast off the virtue he so highly prized,

'And be the very creature he despised?'
"A tenant's wife, half forward, half afraid,
Features, it seem'd, of powerful cast displayed,
That bore down faith and duty; common fame
Speaks of a contract that augments the shame.
"There goes he, not unseen, so strong the will,
And blind the wish, that bear him to the mill;
There he degraded sits, and strives to please
The miller's children, laughing at his knees;
And little Dorcas, now familiar grown,
Talks of her rich papa, and of her own.
He woos the mother's now precarious smile
By costly gifts, that tempers reconcile;
While the rough husband, yielding to the pay
That buys his absence, growling stalks away.
'Tis said th' offending man will sometimes sigh,
And say, 'My God, in what a dream am I!
I will awake;' but, as the day proceeds,
The weaken'd mind the day's indulgence needs;
Hating himself at every step he takes,
His mind approves the virtue he forsakes,
And yet forsakes her. O! how sharp the pain,
Our vice, ourselves, our habits to disdain;
To go where never yet in peace we went;
To feel our hearts can bleed, yet not relent;
To sigh, yet not recede; to grieve, yet not repent!"

TALES OF THE HALL

BOOK IV

ADVENTURES OF RICHARD

Meeting of the Brothers in the Morning—Pictures, Music, Books—The Autumnal Walk—The Farm—The Flock—Effect of Retirement upon the Mind—Dinner—Richard's Adventure at Sea—George inquires into the Education of his Brother—Richard's Account of his Occupations in his early Life: his Pursuits, Associations, Partialities, Affections and Feelings—His Love of Freedom—The Society he chose—The Friendships he engaged in—and the Habits he contracted.

TALES OF THE HALL

BOOK IV

Eight days had past; the Brothers now could meet
With ease, and take the customary seat.
"These" said the host—for he perceived where stray'd
His brother's eye, and what he now survey'd—
"These are the costly trifles that we buy,
Urged by the strong demands of vanity,
The thirst and hunger of a mind diseased,
That must with purchased flattery be appeased;
But yet, 'tis true, the things that you behold
Serve to amuse us as we're getting old.
These pictures, as I heard our artists say,
Are genuine all, and I believe they may;
They cost the genuine sums, and I should grieve
If, being willing, I could not believe.
And there is music; when the ladies come,
With their keen looks they scrutinize the room
To see what pleases, and I must expect
To yield them pleasure, or to find neglect:
For, as attractions from our person fly,
Our purses, Richard, must the want supply;
Yet would it vex me, could the triflers know
That they can shut out comfort or bestow.
"But see this room: here, Richard, you will find
Books for all palates, food for every mind;
This readers term the ever-new delight,
And so it is, if minds have appetite:
Mine once was craving; great my joy, indeed,
Had I possess'd such food when I could feed;
When at the call of every new-born wish
I could have keenly relish'd every dish—
Now, Richard, now, I stalk around and look
Upon the dress and title of a book,
Try half a page, and then can taste no more,
But the dull volume to its place restore;
Begin a second slowly to peruse,
Then cast it by, and look about for news;
The news itself grows dull in long debates—
I skip, and see what the conclusion states;
And many a speech, with zeal and study made
Cold and resisting spirits to persuade,
Is lost on mine; alone, we cease to feel
What crowds admire, and wonder at their zeal.
"But how the day? No fairer will it be?
Walk you? Alas! 'tis requisite for me—
Nay, let me not prescribe—my friends and guests are free."

It was a fair and mild autumnal sky,
And earth's ripe treasures met th' admiring eye,
As a rich beauty, when her bloom is lost,
Appears with more magnificence and cost.
The wet and heavy grass, where feet had stray'd,
Not yet erect, the wanderer's way betray'd;
Showers of the night had swell'd the deep'ning rill;
The morning breeze had urged the quick'ning mill;
Assembled rooks had wing'd their sea-ward flight,
By the same passage to return at night;
While proudly o'er them hung the steady kite,
Then turn'd him back, and left the noisy throng,
Nor deign'd to know them as he sail'd along.
Long yellow leaves from oziers, strew'd around,
Choked the small stream, and hush'd the feeble sound;
While the dead foliage dropt from loftier trees
Our squire beheld not with his wonted ease,
But to his own reflections made reply,
And said aloud, "Yes! doubtless we must die."
"We must;" said Richard, "and we would not live
To feel what dotage and decay will give;
But we yet taste whatever we behold:
The morn is lovely, though the air is cold;
There is delicious quiet in this scene,
At once so rich, so varied, so serene;
Sounds too delight us—each discordant tone
Thus mingled please, that fail to please alone:
This hollow wind, this rustling of the brook,
The farm-yard noise, the woodman at yon oak—
See, the axe falls!—now listen to the stroke!
That gun itself, that murders all this peace,
Adds to the charm, because it soon must cease."
"No doubt," said George, "the country has its charms!
My farm behold! the model for all farms!
Look at that land—you find not there a weed,
We grub the roots, and suffer none to seed.
To land like this no botanist will come,
To seek the precious ware he hides at home;
Pressing the leaves and flowers with effort nice,
As if they came from herbs in Paradise;
Let them their favourites with my neighbours see,
They have no—what?—no habitat with me.
"Now see my flock, and hear its glory;—none
Have that vast body and that slender bone;
They are the village boast, the dealer's theme,
Fleece of such staple! flesh in such esteem!"
"Brother," said Richard, "do I hear aright?
Does the land truly give so much delight?"

"So says my bailiff; sometimes I have tried
To catch the joy, but nature has denied;
It will not be—the mind has had a store
Laid up for life, and will admit no more.
Worn out in trials, and about to die,
In vain to these we for amusement fly;
We farm, we garden, we our poor employ,
And much command, though little we enjoy;
Or, if ambitious, we employ our pen,
We plant a desert, or we drain a fen;
And—here, behold my medal!—this will show
What men may merit when they nothing know."
"Yet reason here," said Richard, "joins with pride:— '
"I did not ask th' alliance," George replied—
"I grant it true, such trifle may induce
A dull, proud man to wake and be of use;
And there are purer pleasures, that a mind
Calm and uninjured may in villas find;
But, where th' affections have been deeply tried,
With other food that mind must be supplied:
'Tis not in trees or medals to impart
The powerful medicine for an aching heart;
The agitation dies, but there is still
The backward spirit, the resisting will.
Man takes his body to a country seat,
But minds, dear Richard, have their own retreat;
Oft when the feet are pacing o'er the green
The mind is gone where never grass was seen,
And never thinks of hill, or vale, or plain,
Till want of rest creates a sense of pain,
That calls that wandering mind, and brings it home again.
No more of farms; but here I boast of minds
That make a friend the richer when he finds:
These shalt thou see;—but, Richard, be it known,
Who thinks to see must in his turn be shown.—
But now farewell! to thee will I resign
Woods, walks, and valleys! take them till we dine."

The Brothers dined, and with that plenteous fare
That seldom fails to dissipate our care,
At least the lighter kind; and oft prevails
When reason, duty, nay, when kindness fails.
Yet food and wine, and all that mortals bless,
Lead them to think of peril and distress—
Cold, hunger, danger, solitude, and pain,
That men in life's adventurous ways sustain.
"Thou hast sail'd far, dear brother," said the 'squire—
"Permit me of these unknown lands t' inquire,

Lands never till'd, where thou hast wondering been,
And all the marvels thou hast heard and seen.
Do tell me something of the miseries felt
In climes where travellers freeze, and where they melt;
And be not nice—we know 'tis not in men
Who travel far to hold a steady pen.
Some will, 'tis true, a bolder freedom take,
And keep our wonder always wide awake;
We know of those whose dangers far exceed
Our frail belief, that trembles as we read:
Such as in deserts burn, and thirst, and die,
Save a last gasp that they recover by;
Then, too, their hazard from a tyrant's arms,
A tiger's fury, or a lady's charms;
Beside th' accumulated evils borne
From the bold outset to the safe return.
These men abuse; but thou hast fair pretence
To modest dealing, and to mild good sense;
Then let me hear thy struggles and escapes
In the far lands of crocodiles and apes:
Say, hast thou, Bruce-like, knelt upon the bed
Where the young Nile uplifts his branchy head?
Or been partaker of th' unhallow'd feast,
Where beast-like man devours his fellow beast,
And churn'd the bleeding life? while each great dame
And sovereign beauty bade adieu to shame?
Or did the storm, that thy wreck'd pinnace bore,
Impel thee gasping on some unknown shore;
Where, when thy beard and nails were savage grown,
Some swarthy princess took thee for her own,
Some danger-dreading Yarico, who, kind,
Sent thee away, and, prudent, staid behind?
"Come—I am ready wonders to receive,
Prone to assent, and willing to believe."
Richard replied: "It must be known to you,
That tales improbable may yet be true;
And yet it is a foolish thing to tell
A tale that shall be judged improbable;
While some impossibilities appear
So like the truth, that we assenting hear:
Yet, with your leave, I venture to relate
A chance-affair, and fact alone will state;
Though, I confess, it may suspicion breed,
And you may cry, 'improbable, indeed!'

"When first I tried the sea, I took a trip,
But duty none, in a relation's ship;
Thus, unengaged, I felt my spirits light,

Kept care at distance, and put fear to flight;
Oft this same spirit in my friends prevail'd,
Buoyant in dangers, rising when assail'd;
When, as the gale at evening died away—
And die it will with the retiring day—
Impatient then, and sick of very ease,
We loudly whistled for the slumbering breeze.
"One eve it came; and, frantic in my joy,
I rose and danced, as idle as a boy:
The cabin-lights were down, that we might learn
A trifling something from the ship astern;
The stiffening gale bore up the growing wave,
And wilder motion to my madness gave.
Oft have I since, when thoughtful and at rest,
Believed some maddening power my mind possess'd;
For, in an instant, as the stern sank low,
(How moved I knew not—What can madness know?)
Chance that direction to my motion gave,
And plunged me headlong in the roaring wave;
Swift flew the parting ship,—the fainter light
Withdrew,—or horror took them from my sight.
"All was confused above, beneath, around;
All sounds of terror; no distinguish'd sound
Could reach me, now on sweeping surges tost,
And then between the rising billows lost
An undefined sensation stopp'd my breath;
Disorder'd views and threat'ning signs of death
Met in one moment, and a terror gave—
I cannot paint it—to the moving grave.
My thoughts were all distressing, hurried, mix'd,
On all things fixing, not a moment fix'd,
Vague thoughts of instant danger brought their pain,
New hopes of safety banish'd them again;
Then the swoln billow all these hopes destroy'd,
And left me sinking in the mighty void.
Weaker I grew, and grew the more dismay'd,
Of aid all hopeless, yet in search of aid;
Struggling awhile upon the wave to keep,
Then, languid, sinking in the yawning deep.
So tost, so lost, so sinking in despair,
I pray'd in heart an indirected prayer,
And then once more I gave my eyes to view
The ship now lost, and bade the light adieu!
From my chill'd frame th' enfeebled spirit fled,
Rose the tall billows round my deep'ning bed,
Cold seized my heart, thought ceased, and I was dead.
"Brother, I have not—man has not, the power
To paint the horrors of that life-long hour—

Hour!—but of time I knew not—when I found
Hope, youth, life, love, and all they promised, drown'd;
When all so indistinct, so undefined,
So dark and dreadful, overcame the mind;
When such confusion on the spirit dwelt,
That, feeling much, it knew not what it felt.
"Can I, my brother—ought I to forget
That night of terror? No! it threatens yet.
Shall I days, months—nay, years indeed neglect,
Who then could feel what moments must effect,
Were aught effected? who, in that wild storm,
Found there was nothing I could well perform;
For what to us are moments, what are hours,
If lost our judgment, and confused our powers?
"Oft in the times when passion strives to reign,
When duty feebly holds the slacken'd chain,
When reason slumbers, then remembrance draws
This view of death, and folly makes a pause—
The view o'ercomes the vice, the fear the frenzy awes.
"I know there wants not this to make it true,
'What danger bids be done, in safety do';
Yet such escapes may make our purpose sure;
Who slights such warning may be too secure."
"But the escape!"—"Whate'er they judged might save
Their sinking friend they cast upon the wave;
Something of these my heaven-directed arm
Unconscious seized, and held as by a charm;
The crew astern beheld me as I swam,
And I am saved—O! let me say I am."

"Brother," said George, "I have neglected long
To think of all thy perils—it was wrong;
But do forgive me; for I could not be
Than of myself more negligent of thee.
Now tell me, Richard, from the boyish years
Of thy young mind, that now so rich appears,
How was it stored? 'twas told me, thou wert wild,
A truant urchin, a neglected child.
I heard of this escape, and sat supine
Amid the danger that exceeded thine;
Thou couldst but die—the waves could but infold
Thy warm, gay heart, and make that bosom cold—
While I—but no! Proceed, and give me truth;
How past the years of thy unguided youth?
Thy father left thee to the care of one
Who could not teach, could ill support a son;
Yet time and trouble feeble minds have stay'd,
And fit for long-neglected duties made.

I see thee struggling in the world, as late
Within the waves, and, with an equal fate,
By Heaven preserved—but tell me, whence and how
Thy gleaning came?—a dexterous gleaner thou!"
"Left by that father, who was known to few,
And to that mother, who has not her due
Of honest fame," said Richard, "our retreat
Was a small cottage, for our station meet,
On Barford Downs; that mother, fond and poor,
There taught some truths, and bade me seek for more,
Such as our village-school and books a few
Supplied; but such I cared not to pursue.
I sought the town, and to the ocean gave
My mind and thoughts, as restless as the wave;
Where crowds assembled, I was sure to run,
Hear[c] what was said, and mused on what was done;
Attentive listening in the moving scene,
And often wondering what the men could mean.
"When ships at sea made signals of their need,
I watch'd on shore the sailors, and their speed;
Mix'd in their act, nor rested till I knew
Why they were call'd, and what they were to do.
"Whatever business in the port was done,
I, without call, was with the busy one;
Not daring question, but with open ear
And greedy spirit, ever bent to hear.
"To me the wives of seamen loved to tell
What storms endanger'd men esteem'd so well;
What wond'rous things in foreign parts they saw,
Lands without bounds, and people without law.
"No ships were wreck'd upon that fatal beach,
But I could give the luckless tale of each;
Eager I look'd, till I beheld a face
Of one disposed to paint their dismal case;
Who gave the sad survivors' doleful tale,
From the first brushing of the mighty gale
Until they struck; and, suffering in their fate,
I long'd the more they should its horrors state;
While some, the fond of pity, would enjoy
The earnest sorrows of the feeling boy.
"I sought the men return'd from regions cold,
The frozen straits, where icy mountains roll'd;
Some I could win to tell me serious tales
Of boats uplifted by enormous whales,
Or, when harpoon'd, how swiftly through the sea
The wounded monsters with the cordage flee.
Yet some uneasy thoughts assail'd me then:
The monsters warr'd not with, nor wounded, men.

The smaller fry we take, with scales and fins,
Who gasp and die—this adds not to our sins;
But so much blood, warm life, and frames so large
To strike, to murder—seem'd an heavy charge.
"They told of days, where many goes to one—
Such days as ours; and how a larger sun,
Red, but not flaming, roll'd, with motion slow,
On the world's edge, and never dropt below.
"There were fond girls, who took me to their side
To tell the story how their lovers died;
They praised my tender heart, and bade me prove
Both kind and constant when I came to love.
In fact, I lived for many an idle year
In fond pursuit of agitations dear;
For ever seeking, ever pleased to find,
The food I loved, I thought not of its kind;
It gave affliction while it brought delight,
And joy and anguish could at once excite.
"One gusty day, now stormy and now still,
I stood apart upon the western hill,
And saw a race at sea: a gun was heard,
And two contending boats in sail appear'd,
Equal awhile; then one was left behind,
And for a moment had her chance resign'd,
When, in that moment, up a sail they drew—
Not used before—their rivals to pursue.
Strong was the gale! in hurry now there came
Men from the town, their thoughts, their fears the same;
And women too! affrighted maids and wives,
All deeply feeling for their sailors' lives.
"The strife continued; in a glass we saw
The desperate efforts, and we stood in awe:
When the last boat shot suddenly before,
Then fill'd, and sank—and could be seen no more!
"Then were those piercing shrieks, that frantic flight,
All hurried! all in tumult and affright!
A gathering crowd from different streets drew near;
All ask, all answer—none attend, none hear!
"One boat is safe; and see! she backs her sail
To save the sinking—Will her care avail?
"O! how impatient on the sands we tread,
And the winds roaring, and the women led,
As up and down they pace with frantic air,
And scorn a comforter, and will despair;
They know not who in either boat is gone,
But think the father, husband, lover, one.
"And who is she apart? She dares not come
To join the crowd, yet cannot rest at home:

With what strong interest looks she at the waves,
Meeting and clashing o'er the seamen's graves:
'Tis a poor girl betroth'd—a few hours more,
And he will lie a corpse upon the shore.
"Strange, that a boy could love these scenes, and cry
In very pity—but that boy was I.
With pain my mother would my tales receive,
And say, 'my Richard, do not learn to grieve.'
"One wretched hour had past before we knew
Whom they had saved! Alas! they were but two,
An orphan'd lad and widow'd man—no more!
And they unnoticed stood upon the shore,
With scarce a friend to greet them—widows view'd
This man and boy, and then their cries renew'd;—
'Twas long before the signs of wo gave place
To joy again; grief sat on every face.
"Sure of my mother's kindness, and the joy
She felt in meeting her rebellious boy,
I at my pleasure our new seat forsook,
And, undirected, these excursions took:
I often rambled to the noisy quay,
Strange sounds to hear, and business strange to me;
Seamen and carmen, and I know not who,
A lewd, amphibious, rude, contentious crew—
Confused as bees appear about their hive,
Yet all alert to keep their work alive.
"Here, unobserved as weed upon the wave,
My whole attention to the scene I gave;
I saw their tasks, their toil, their care, their skill,
Led by their own and by a master-will;
And, though contending, toiling, tugging on,
The purposed business of the day was done.
"The open shops of craftsmen caught my eye,
And there my questions met the kind reply:
Men, when alone, will teach; but, in a crowd,
The child is silent, or the man is proud;
But, by themselves, there is attention paid
To a mild boy, so forward, yet afraid.
"I made me interest at the inn's fire-side,
Amid the scenes to bolder boys denied;
For I had patrons there, and I was one,
They judged, who noticed nothing that was done.
'A quiet lad!' would my protector say;
'To him, now, this is better than his play:
Boys are as men; some active, shrewd, and keen,
They look about if aught is to be seen;
And some, like Richard here, have not a mind
That takes a notice—but the lad is kind.'

"I loved in summer on the heath to walk,
And seek the shepherd—shepherds love to talk.
His superstition was of ranker kind,
And he with tales of wonder stored my mind;
Wonders that he in many a lonely eve
Had seen, himself, and therefore must believe.
His boy, his Joe, he said, from duty ran,
Took to the sea, and grew a fearless man:
'On yonder knoll—the sheep were in the fold—
His spirit past me, shivering-like and cold!
I felt a fluttering, but I knew not how,
And heard him utter, like a whisper, 'now!'
Soon came a letter from a friend—to tell
That he had fallen, and the time he fell.'
"Even to the smugglers' hut the rocks between,
I have, adventurous in my wandering, been.
Poor, pious Martha served the lawless tribe,
And could their merits and their faults describe;
Adding her thoughts; 'I talk, my child, to you,
Who little think of what such wretches do.'
"I loved to walk where none had walk'd before,
About the rocks that ran along the shore;
Or far beyond the sight of men to stray,
And take my pleasure when I lost my way;
For then 'twas mine to trace the hilly heath,
And all the mossy moor that lies beneath:
Here had I favourite stations, where I stood
And heard the murmurs of the ocean-flood,
With not a sound beside, except when flew
Aloft the lapwing, or the gray curlew,
Who with wild notes my fancied power defied,
And mock'd the dreams of solitary pride.
"I loved to stop at every creek and bay
Made by the river in its winding way,
And call to memory—not by marks they bare,
But by the thoughts that were created there.
"Pleasant it was to view the sea-gulls strive
Against the storm, or in the ocean dive,
With eager scream, or when they dropping gave
Their closing wings to sail upon the wave:
Then, as the winds and waters raged around,
And breaking billows mix'd their deafening sound,
They on the rolling deep securely hung,
And calmly rode the restless waves among.
Nor pleased it less around me to behold,
Far up the beach, the yesty sea-foam roll'd;
Or, from the shore upborn, to see on high
Its frothy flakes in wild confusion fly;

While the salt spray that clashing billows form,
Gave to the taste a feeling of the storm.
"Thus, with my favourite views, for many an hour
Have I indulged the dreams of princely power;
When the mind, weaned by excursions bold,
The fancy jaded, and the bosom cold,
Or when those wants that will on kings intrude,
Or evening-fears, broke in on solitude;
When I no more my fancy could employ,
I left in haste what I could not enjoy,
And was my gentle mother's welcome boy.
"But now thy walk,—this soft autumnal gloom
Bids no delay—at night I will resume
My subject, showing, not how I improved
In my strange school, but what the things I loved,
My first-born friendships, ties by forms uncheck'd,
And all that boys acquire whom men neglect."

TALES OF THE HALL

BOOK V

RUTH

Richard resumes his Narrative—Visits a Family in a Seaport—The Man and his Wife—Their Dwelling—
Books, Number and Kind—The Friendship contracted—Employment there—Hannah, the Wife, her
Manner; open Mirth and latent Grief—She gives the Story of Ruth, her Daughter—Of Thomas, a Sailor—
Their Affection—A Press-gang— Reflections—Ruth disturbed in Mind—A Teacher sent to comfort her—
His Fondness—Her Reception of him—Her Supplication—Is refused—She deliberates—Is decided.

TALES OF THE HALL

BOOK V

RUTH

Richard would wait till George the tale should ask,
Nor waited long—He then resumed the task.
"South in the port, and eastward in the street,
Rose a small dwelling, my beloved retreat,
Where lived a pair, then old; the sons had fled

The home they fill'd; a part of them were dead,
Married a part, while some at sea remain'd,
And stillness in the seaman's mansion reign'd;
Lord of some petty craft, by night and day,
The man had fish'd each fathom of the bay.
"My friend the matron woo'd me, quickly won,
To fill the station of an absent son
(Him whom at school I knew, and, Peter known,
I took his home and mother for my own).
I read, and doubly was I paid to hear
Events that fell upon no listless ear:
She grieved to say her parents could neglect
Her education!—'twas a sore defect;
She, who had ever such a vast delight
To learn, and now could neither read nor write:—
But hear she could, and from our stores I took,
Librarian meet! at her desire our book.
Full twenty volumes—I would not exceed
The modest truth—were there for me to read;
These a long shelf contain'd, and they were found
Books truly speaking, volumes fairly bound;
The rest—for some of other kinds remain'd,
And these a board beneath the shelf contain'd—
Had their deficiencies in part; they lack'd
One side or both, or were no longer back'd;
But now became degraded from their place,
And were but pamphlets of a bulkier race.
Yet had we pamphlets, an inviting store,
From sixpence downwards—nay, a part were more;
Learning abundance, and the various kinds
For relaxation—food for different minds;
A piece of Wingate—thanks for all we have—
What we of figures needed, fully gave;
Culpepper, new in numbers, cost but thrice
The ancient volume's unassuming price,
But told what planet o'er each herb had power,
And how to take it in the lucky hour.
"History we had—wars, treasons, treaties, crimes,
From Julius Cæsar to the present times;
Questions and answers, teaching what to ask
And what reply—a kind, laborious task;
A scholar's book it was, who, giving, swore
It held the whole he wish'd to know, and more.
"And we had poets, hymns and songs divine;
The most we read not, but allow'd them fine.
"Our tracts were many, on the boldest themes—
We had our metaphysics, spirits, dreams,
Visions and warnings, and portentous sights

Seen, though but dimly, in the doleful nights,
When the good wife her wintry vigil keeps,
And thinks alone of him at sea, and weeps.
"Add to all these our works in single sheets,
That our Cassandras sing about the streets.
These, as I read, the grave good man would say,
'Nay, Hannah!' and she answer'd 'What is Nay?
What is there, pray, so hurtful in a song?
It is our fancy only makes it wrong;
His purer mind no evil thoughts alarm,
And innocence protects him like a charm.'
Then would the matron, when the song had past,
And her laugh over, ask an hymn at last;
To the coarse jest she would attention lend,
And to the pious psalm in reverence bend.
She gave her every power and all her mind
As chance directed, or as taste inclined.
"More of our learning I will now omit:
We had our Cyclopædias of Wit,
And all our works, rare fate, were to our genius fit.
"When I had read, and we were weary grown
Of other minds, the dame disclosed her own;
And long have I in pleasing terror stay'd
To hear of boys trepann'd, and girls betray'd;
Ashamed so long to stay, and yet to go afraid.
"I could perceive, though Hannah bore full well
The ills of life, that few with her would dwell,
But pass away, like shadows o'er the plain
From flying clouds, and leave it fair again;
Still every evil, be it great or small,
Would one past sorrow to the mind recal—
The grand disease of life, to which she turns,
And common cares and lighter suffering spurns.
'O! these are nothing,—they will never heed
Such idle contests who have fought indeed,
And have the wounds unclosed.'—I understood
My hint to speak, and my design pursued,
Curious the secret of that heart to find,
To mirth, to song, to laughter loud inclined,
And yet to bear and feel a weight of grief behind.
How does she thus her little sunshine throw
Always before her?—I should like to know.
My friend perceived, and would no longer hide
The bosom's sorrow—Could she not confide
In one who wept, unhurt—in one who felt, untried?
'Dear child, I show you sins and sufferings strange,
But you, like Adam, must for knowledge change
That blissful ignorance: remember, then,

What now you feel should be a check on men;
For then your passions no debate allow,
And therefore lay up resolution now.
'Tis not enough, that when you can persuade
A maid to love, you know there's promise made;
'Tis not enough, that you design to keep
That promise made, nor leave your lass to weep:
But you must guard yourself against the sin,
And think it such to draw the party in;
Nay, the more weak and easy to be won,
The viler you who have the mischief done.
I am not angry, love; but men should know
They cannot always pay the debt they owe
Their plighted honour; they may cause the ill
They cannot lessen, though they feel a will;
For he had truth with love, but love in youth
Does wrong, that cannot be repair'd by truth.
Ruth—I may tell, too oft had she been told—
Was tall and fair, and comely to behold;
Gentle and simple, in her native place
Not one compared with her in form or face;
She was not merry, but she gave our hearth
A cheerful spirit that was more than mirth.
There was a sailor boy, and people said
He was, as man, a likeness of the maid;
But not in this—for he was ever glad,
While Ruth was apprehensive, mild, and sad;
A quiet spirit hers, and peace would seek
In meditation—tender, mild, and meek!
Her loved the lad most truly; and, in truth,
She took an early liking to the youth;
To her alone were his attentions paid,
And they became the bachelor and maid.
He wish'd to marry; but so prudent we
And worldly wise, we said it could not be.
They took the counsel—may be they approved—
But still they grieved and waited, hoped and loved.
Now, my young friend, when of such state I speak
As one of danger, you will be to seek:
You know not, Richard, where the danger lies
In loving hearts, kind words, and speaking eyes;
For lovers speak their wishes with their looks
As plainly, love, as you can read your books.
Then, too, the meetings and the partings, all
The playful quarrels in which lovers fall,
Serve to one end—each lover is a child,
Quick to resent and to be reconciled;
And then their peace brings kindness that remains,

And so the lover from the quarrel gains.
When he has fault that she reproves, his fear
And grief assure her she was too severe:
And that brings kindness—when he bears an ill,
Or disappointment, and is calm and still,
She feels his own obedient to her will:
And that brings kindness—and what kindness brings
I cannot tell you;—these were trying things.
They were as children, and they fell at length;
The trial, doubtless, is beyond their strength
Whom grace supports not; and will grace support
The too confiding, who their danger court?
Then they would marry—but were now too late—
All could their fault in sport or malice state;
And though the day was fix'd, and now drew on,
I could perceive my daughter's peace was gone;
She could not bear the bold and laughing eye
That gazed on her—reproach she could not fly;
Her grief she would not show, her shame could not deny;
For some with many virtues come to shame,
And some that lose them all preserve their name.
"'Fix'd was the day; but ere that day appear'd,
A frightful rumour through the place was heard;
War, who had slept awhile, awaked once more,
And gangs came pressing till they swept the shore:
Our youth was seized and quickly sent away,
Nor would the wretches for his marriage stay,
But bore him off, in barbarous triumph bore,
And left us all our miseries to deplore.
There were wives, maids, and mothers on the beach,
And some sad story appertain'd to each;
Most sad to Ruth—to neither could she go!
But sat apart, and suffer'd matchless wo!
On the vile ship they turn'd their earnest view,
Not one last [look] allow'd,—not one adieu!
They saw the men on deck, but none distinctly knew.
And there she staid, regardless of each eye,
With but one hope, a fervent hope to die.
Nor cared she now for kindness—all beheld
Her, who invited none, and none repell'd;
For there are griefs, my child, that sufferers hide,
And there are griefs that men display with pride;
But there are other griefs that, so we feel,
We care not to display them nor conceal:
Such were our sorrows on that fatal day,
More than our lives the spoilers tore away;
Nor did we heed their insult—some distress
No form or manner can make more or less,

And this is of that kind—this misery of a press!
'They say such things must be—perhaps they must;
But, sure, they need not fright us and disgust;
They need not soul-less crews of ruffians send
At once the ties of humble love to rend.
A single day had Thomas stay'd on shore,
He might have wedded, and we ask'd no more;
And that stern man, who forced the lad away,
Might have attended, and have graced the day;
His pride and honour might have been at rest,
It is no stain to make a couple blest!
Blest!—no, alas! it was to ease the heart
Of one sore pang, and then to weep and part!
But this he would not.—English seamen fight
For England's gain and glory—it is right;
But will that public spirit be so strong,
Fill'd, as it must be, with their private wrong?
Forbid it, honour, one in all the fleet
Should hide in war, or from the foe retreat!
But is it just, that he who so defends
His country's cause, should hide him from her friends?
Sure, if they must upon our children seize,
They might prevent such injuries as these;
Might hours—nay, days—in many a case allow,
And soften all the griefs we suffer now.
Some laws, some orders might in part redress
The licensed insults of a British press,
That keeps the honest and the brave in awe,
Where might is right, and violence is law.
'Be not alarm'd, my child; there's none regard
What you and I conceive so cruel-hard:
There is compassion, I believe; but still
One wants the power to help, and one the will,
And so from war to war the wrongs remain,
While Reason pleads, and Misery sighs, in vain.
'Thus my poor Ruth was wretched and undone,
Nor had an husband for her only son,
Nor had he father; hope she did awhile,
And would not weep, although she could not smile;
Till news was brought us that the youth was slain,
And then, I think, she never smiled again;
Or if she did, it was but to express
A feeling far, indeed, from happiness!
Something that her bewilder'd mind conceived,
When she inform'd us that she never grieved,
But was right merry, then her head was wild,
And grief had gain'd possession of my child.
Yet, though bewilder'd for a time, and prone

To ramble much and speak aloud, alone;
Yet did she all that duty ever ask'd
And more, her will self-govern'd and untask'd.
With meekness bearing all reproach, all joy
To her was lost; she wept upon her boy,
Wish'd for his death, in fear that he might live
New sorrow to a burden'd heart to give.
'There was a teacher, where my husband went—
Sent, as he told the people—what he meant
You cannot understand, but—he was sent.
This man from meeting came, and strove to win
Her mind to peace by drawing off the sin,
Or what it was, that, working in her breast,
Robb'd it of comfort, confidence, and rest.
He came and reason'd, and she seem'd to feel
The pains he took—her griefs began to heal;
She ever answer'd kindly when he spoke,
And always thank'd him for the pains he took;
So, after three long years, and all the while
Wrapt up in grief, she blest us with a smile,
And spoke in comfort; but she mix'd no more
With younger persons, as she did before.
'Still Ruth was pretty; in her person neat;
So thought the teacher, when they chanced to meet.
He was a weaver by his worldly trade,
But powerful work in the assemblies made;
People came leagues to town to hear him sift
The holy text,—he had the grace and gift;
Widows and maidens flock'd to hear his voice;
Of either kind he might have had his choice;—
But he had chosen—we had seen how shy
The girl was getting, my good man and I;
That when the weaver came, she kept with us,
Where he his points and doctrines might discuss;
But in our bit of garden, or the room
We call our parlour, there he must not come.
She loved him not, and though she could attend
To his discourses as her guide and friend,
Yet now to these she gave a listless ear,
As if a friend she would no longer hear;
This might he take for woman's art, and cried,
'Spouse of my heart, I must not be denied!'—
Fearless he spoke, and I had hope to see
My girl a wife—but this was not to be.
'My husband, thinking of his worldly store,
And not, frail man, enduring to be poor,
Seeing his friend would for his child provide
And hers, he grieved to have the man denied;

For Ruth, when press'd, rejected him, and grew
To her old sorrow, as if that were new.
'Who shall support her?' said her father, 'how
Can I, infirm and weak as I am now?
And here a loving fool'—this gave her pain
Severe, indeed, but she would not complain;
Nor would consent, although the weaver grew
More fond, and would the frighten'd girl pursue.
'O! much she begg'd him to forbear, to stand
Her soul's kind friend, and not to ask her hand:
She could not love him.—'Love me!' he replied,
'The love you mean is love unsanctified,
An earthly, wicked, sensual, sinful kind,
A creature-love, the passion of the blind.'
He did not court her, he would have her know,
For that poor love that will on beauty grow;
No! he would take her as the prophet took
One of the harlots in the holy book;
And then he look'd so ugly and severe!
And yet so fond—she could not hide her fear.
This fondness grew her torment; she would fly
In woman's terror, if he came but nigh;
Nor could I wonder he should odious prove,
So like a ghost that left a grave for love.
But still her father lent his cruel aid
To the man's hope, and she was more afraid:
He said, no more she should his table share,
But be the parish or the teacher's care.
'Three days I give you: see that all be right
On Monday-morning—this is Thursday-night—
Fulfil my wishes, girl! or else forsake my sight!'
'I see her now; and, she that was so meek
It was a chance that she had power to speak,
Now spoke in earnest—'Father! I obey,
And will remember the appointed day!'
'Then came the man: she talk'd with him apart,
And, I believe, laid open all her heart;
But all in vain—she said to me, in tears,
'Mother! that man is not what he appears:
He talks of heaven, and let him, if he will,
But he has earthly purpose to fulfil;
Upon my knees I begg'd him to resign
The hand he asks—he said, 'it shall be mine.
'What! did the holy men of Scripture deign
To hear a woman when she said 'refrain?'
Of whom they chose they took them wives, and these
Made it their study and their wish to please;
The women then were faithful and afraid,

As Sarah Abraham, they their lords obey'd,
And so she styled him; 'tis in later days
Of foolish love that we our women praise,
Fall on the knee, and raise the suppliant hand,
And court the favour that we might command.'
O! my dear mother, when this man has power,
How will he treat me—first may beasts devour!
Or death in every form that I could prove,
Except this selfish being's hateful love.'
I gently blamed her, for I knew how hard
It is to force affection and regard.
Ah! my dear lad, I talk to you as one
Who knew the misery of an heart undone;
You know it not; but, dearest boy, when man,
Do not an ill because you find you can.
Where is the triumph? when such things men seek,
They only drive to wickedness the weak.
Weak was poor Ruth, and this good man so hard,
That to her weakness he had no regard;
But we had two days peace; he came, and then
My daughter whisper'd, 'Would there were no men
None to admire or scorn us, none to vex
A simple, trusting, fond, believing sex;
Who truly love the worth that men profess,
And think too kindly for their happiness.'
Poor Ruth! few heroines in the tragic page
Felt more than thee in thy contracted stage;
Fair, fond, and virtuous, they our pity move,
Impell'd by duty, agonized by love;
But no Mandane, who in dread has knelt
On the bare boards, has greater terrors felt,
Nor been by warring passions more subdued
Than thou, by this man's groveling wish pursued;
Doom'd to a parent's judgment, all unjust,
Doom'd the chance mercy of the world to trust,
Or to wed grossness and conceal disgust.
If Ruth was frail, she had a mind too nice
To wed with that which she beheld as vice;
To take a reptile, who, beneath a show
Of peevish zeal, let carnal wishes grow;
Proud and yet mean, forbidding and yet full
Of eager appetites, devout and dull;
Waiting a legal right that he might seize
His own, and his impatient spirit ease;
Who would at once his pride and love indulge,
His temper humour, and his spite divulge.
This the poor victim saw—a second time,
Sighing, she said, 'Shall I commit the crime,

And now untempted? Can the form or rite
Make me a wife in my Creator's sight?
Can I the words without a meaning say?
Can I pronounce love, honour, or obey?
And if I cannot, shall I dare to wed,
And go an harlot to a loathed bed?
Never, dear mother! my poor boy and I
Will at the mercy of a parish lie:
Reproved for wants that vices would remove,
Reproach'd for vice that I could never love,
Mix'd with a crew long wedded to disgrace,
A Vulgar, forward, equalizing race—
And am I doom'd to beg a dwelling in that place?'
Such was her reasoning: many times she weigh'd
The evils all, and was of each afraid;
She loath'd the common board, the vulgar seat,
Where shame, and want, and vice, and sorrow meet,
Where frailty finds allies, where guilt insures retreat.
But peace again is fled; the teacher comes,
And new importance, haughtier air assumes.
No hapless victim of a tyrant's love
More keenly felt, or more resisting strove
Against her fate; she look'd on every side,
But there were none to help her, none to guide;—
And he, the man who should have taught the soul,
Wish'd but the body in his base control.
She left her infant on the Sunday morn,
A creature doom'd to shame! in sorrow born;
A thing that languished, nor arrived at age
When the man's thoughts with sin and pain engage—
She came not home to share our humble meal,
Her father thinking what his child would feel
From his hard sentence—still she came not home.
The night grew dark, and yet she was not come;
The east-wind roar'd, the sea return'd the sound,
And the rain fell as if the world were drown'd;
There were no lights without, and my good man,
To kindness frighten'd, with a groan began
To talk of Ruth, and pray; and then he took
The Bible down, and read the holy book;
For he had learning; and when that was done
We sat in silence—whither could we run?
We said, and then rush'd frighten'd from the door,
For we could bear our own conceit no more;
We call'd on neighbours—there she had not been;
We met some wanderers—ours they had not seen;
We hurried o'er the beach, both north and south,
Then join'd, and wander'd to our haven's mouth,

Where rush'd the falling waters wildly out:
I scarcely heard the good man's fearful shout,
Who saw a something on the billow ride,
And 'Heaven have mercy on our sins!' he cried,
'It is my child!' and to the present hour
So he believes—and spirits have the power.
And she was gone! the waters wide and deep
Roll'd o'er her body as she lay asleep.
She heard no more the angry waves and wind,
She heard no more the threatening of mankind;
Wrapt in dark weeds, the refuse of the storm,
To the hard rock was borne her comely form!
But O! what storm was in that mind? what strife,
That could compel her to lay down her life?
For she was seen within the sea to wade,
By one at distance, when she first had pray'd;
Then to a rock within the hither shoal
Softly and with a fearful step she stole;
Then, when she gain'd it, on the top she stood
A moment still—and dropt into the flood!
The man cried loudly, but he cried in vain—
She heard not then—she never heard again!
She had—pray, Heav'n!—she had that world in sight,
Where frailty mercy finds, and wrong has right;
But, sure, in this her portion such has been,
Well had it still remain'd a world unseen!
Thus far the dame: the passions will dispense
To such a wild and rapid eloquence—
Will to the weakest mind their strength impart,
And give the tongue the language of the heart."

TALES OF THE HALL

BOOK VI

ADVENTURES OF RICHARD, CONCLUDED

Richard relates his Illness and Retirement—A Village Priest and his two Daughters—His peculiar Studies—His Simplicity of Character—Arrival of a third Daughter—Her Zeal in his Conversion— Their Friendship—How terminated—An happy Day—Its Commencement and Progress—A Journey along the Coast—Arrival as a Guest— Company—A Lover's Jealousy—it increases—dies away—An Evening Walk—Suspense— Apprehension—Resolution—Certainty.

ADVENTURES OF RICHARD, CONCLUDED

"This then, dear Richard, was the way you took
To gain instruction—thine a curious book,
Containing much of both the false and true;
But thou hast read it, and with profit too.
"Come, then, my Brother, now thy tale complete—
I know thy first embarking in the fleet,
Thy entrance in the army, and thy gain
Of plenteous laurels in the wars in Spain,
And what then follow'd; but I wish to know
When thou that heart hadst courage to bestow,
When to declare it gain'd, and when to stand
Before the priest, and give the plighted hand;
So shall I boldness from thy frankness gain
To paint the frenzy that possessed my brain;
For rather there than in my heart I found
Was my disease; a poison, not a wound,
A madness, Richard—but, I pray thee, tell
Whom hast thou loved so dearly and so well?"
The younger man his gentle host obey'd,
For some respect, though not required, was paid;
Perhaps with all that independent pride
Their different states would to the memory glide;
Yet was his manner unconstrain'd and free,
And nothing in it like servility.
Then he began:—"When first I reach'd the land,
I was so ill that death appear'd at hand;
And, though the fever left me, yet I grew
So weak 'twas judged that life would leave me too.
I sought a village-priest, my mother's friend,
And I believed with him my days would end:
The man was kind, intelligent, and mild,
Careless and shrewd, yet simple as the child;
For of the wisdom of the world his share
And mine were equal—neither had to spare;
Else—with his daughters, beautiful and poor—
He would have kept a sailor from his door.
Two then were present, who adorn'd his home,
But ever speaking of a third to come;
Cheerful they were, not too reserved or free,
I loved them both, and never wish'd them three.
"The vicar's self, still further to describe,
Was of a simple, but a studious tribe;

He from the world was distant, not retired,
Nor of it much possess'd, nor much desired:
Grave in his purpose, cheerful in his eye,
And with a look of frank benignity.
He lost his wife when they together past
Years of calm love, that triumph'd to the last.
He much of nature, not of man, had seen,
Yet his remarks were often shrewd and keen;
Taught not by books t' approve or to condemn,
He gain'd but little that he knew from them;
He read with reverence and respect the few,
Whence he his rules and consolations drew;
But men and beasts, and all that lived or moved,
Were books to him; he studied them and loved.
"He knew the plants in mountain, wood, or mead;
He knew the worms that on the foliage feed;
Knew the small tribes that 'scape the careless eye,
The plant's disease that breeds the embryo-fly;
And the small creatures who on bark or bough
Enjoy their changes, changed we know not how;
But now th' imperfect being scarcely moves,
And now takes wing and seeks the sky it loves.
"He had no system, and forbore to read
The learned labours of th' immortal Swede;
But smiled to hear the creatures he had known
So long, were now in class and order shown,
Genus and species—'is it meet,' said he,
'This creature's name should one so sounding be?
Tis but a fly, though first-born of the spring—
Bombylius majus, dost thou call the thing?
Majus, indeed! and yet, in fact, 'tis true,
We all are majors, all are minors too,
Except the first and last—th' immensely distant twc.
And here again—what call the learned this?
Both Hippobosca and Hirundinis?
Methinks the creature should be proud to find
That he employs the talents of mankind;
And that his sovereign master shrewdly looks,
Counts all his parts, and puts them in his books.
Well! go thy way, for I do feel it shame
To stay a being with so proud a name.'
"Such were his daughters, such my quiet friend,
And pleasant was it thus my days to spend;
But when Matilda at her home I saw,
Whom I beheld with anxiousness and awe,
The ease and quiet that I found before
At once departed, and return'd no more.
No more their music soothed me as they play'd,

But soon her words a strong impression made:
The sweet enthusiast, so I deem'd her, took
My mind, and fix'd it to her speech and look;
My soul, dear girl! she made her constant care,
But never whisper'd to my heart 'beware!'
In love no dangers rise till we are in the snare.
Her father sometimes question'd of my creed,
And seem'd to think it might amendment need;
But great the difference when the pious maid
To the same errors her attention paid:
Her sole design that I should think aright,
And my conversion her supreme delight.
Pure was her mind, and simple her intent,
Good all she sought, and kindness all she meant.
Next to religion friendship was our theme,
Related souls and their refined esteem.
We talk'd of scenes where this is real found,
And love subsists without a dart or wound;
But there intruded thoughts not all serene,
And wishes not so calm would intervene."
"Saw not her father?"
"Yes; but saw no more
Than he had seen without a fear before:
He had subsisted by the church and plough,
And saw no cause for apprehension now.
We, too, could live; he thought not passion wrong,
But only wonder'd we delay'd so long.
More had he wonder'd had he known esteem
Was all we mention'd, friendship was our theme.—
Laugh, if you please, I must my tale pursue—
This sacred friendship thus in secret grew
An intellectual love, most tender, chaste, and true;
Unstain'd, we said; nor knew we how it chanced
To gain some earthly soil as it advanced;
But yet my friend, and she alone, could prove
How much it differ'd from romantic love—
But this and more I pass—No doubt, at length,
We could perceive the weakness of our strength.
"O! days remember'd well! remember'd all!
The bitter-sweet, the honey and the gall;
Those garden rambles in the silent night,
Those trees so shady, and that moon so bright;
That thickset alley, by the arbour closed,
That woodbine seat where we at last reposed;
And then the hopes that came and then were gone,
Quick as the clouds beneath the moon passed on.
Now, in this instant, shall my love be shown,
I said—O! no, the happy time is flown!

"You smile; remember, I was weak and low,
And fear'd the passion as I felt it grow:
Will she, I said, to one so poor attend,
Without a prospect, and without a friend?
I dared not ask her—till a rival came,
But hid the secret, slow-consuming flame.
I once had seen him; then familiar, free,
More than became a common guest to be;
And sure, I said, he has a look of pride
And inward joy—a lover satisfied.
Can you not, Brother, on adventures past
A thought, as on a lively prospect, cast?
On days of dear remembrance! days that seem,
When past—nay, even when present—like a dream?
These white and blessed days, that softly shine
On few, nor oft on them—have they been thine?"
George answer'd, "Yes! dear Richard, through the years
Long past, a day so white and mark'd appears.
As in the storm that pours destruction round,
Is here and there a ship in safety found:
So in the storms of life some days appear
More blest and bright for the preceding fear.
These times of pleasure that in life arise,
Like spots in deserts, that delight, surprise,
And to our wearied senses give the more,
For all the waste behind us and before—
And thou, dear Richard, hast then had thy share
Of those enchanting times that baffle care?"
Yes, I have felt this life-refreshing gale
That bears us onward when our spirits fail;
That gives those spirits vigour and delight—
I would describe it, could I do it right.
Such days have been—a day of days was one
When, rising gaily with the rising sun,
I took my way to join a happy few,
Known not to me, but whom Matilda knew,
To whom she went a guest, and message sent:
Come thou to us;' and as a guest I went.
There are two ways to Brandon—by the heath
Above the cliff, or on the sand beneath,
Where the small pebbles, wetted by the wave,
To the new day reflected lustre gave.
At first above the rocks I made my way,
Delighted looking at the spacious bay,
And the large fleet that to the northward steer'd
Full sail, that glorious in my view appear'd;
For where does man evince his full control
O'er subject matter, where displays the soul

Its mighty energies with more effect
Than when her powers that moving mass direct?
Than when man guides the ship man's art has made,
And makes the winds and waters yield him aid?
"Much as I long'd to see the maid I loved,
Through scenes so glorious I at leisure moved;
For there are times when we do not obey
The master-passion—when we yet delay—
When absence, soon to end, we yet prolong,
And dally with our wish although so strong.
"High were my joys, but they were sober too,
Nor reason spoil'd the pictures fancy drew;
I felt—rare feeling in a world like this—
The sober certainty of waking bliss;
Add too the smaller aids to happy men,
Convenient helps—these too were present then.
"But what are spirits? light indeed and gay
They are, like winter flowers, nor last a day;
Comes a rude icy wind—they feel, and fade away.
"High beat my heart when to the house I came,
And when the ready servant gave my name;
But when I enter'd that pernicious room,
Gloomy it look'd, and painful was the gloom;
And jealous was the pain, and deep the sigh
Caused by this gloom, and pain, and jealousy:
For there Matilda sat, and her beside
That rival soldier, with a soldier's pride;
With self-approval in his laughing face,
His seem'd the leading spirit of the place.
She was all coldness—yet I thought a look,
But that corrected, tender welcome spoke:
It was as lightning which you think you see,
But doubt, and ask if lightning it could be.
"Confused and quick my introduction pass'd,
When I, a stranger and on strangers cast,
Beheld the gallant man as he display'd
Uncheck'd attention to the guilty maid.
O! how it grieved me that she dared t' excite
Those looks in him that show'd so much delight;
Egregious coxcomb! there—he smiled again,
As if he sought to aggravate my pain;
Still she attends—I must approach—and find,
Or make, a quarrel, to relieve my mind.
"In vain I try—politeness as a shield
The angry strokes of my contempt repell'd;
Nor must I violate the social law
That keeps the rash and insolent in awe.
Once I observed, on hearing my replies,

The woman's terror fix'd on me the eyes
That look'd entreaty; but the guideless rage
Of jealous minds no softness can assuage.
But, lo! they rise, and all prepare to take
The promised pleasure on the neighbouring lake.
"Good heaven! they whisper! Is it come to this?
Already!—then may I my doubt dismiss:
Could he so soon a timid girl persuade?
What rapid progress has the coxcomb made!
And yet how cool her looks, and how demure!
The falling snow nor lily's flower so pure—
What can I do? I must the pair attend,
And watch this horrid business to its end.
"There, forth they go! He leads her to the shore—
Nay, I must follow—I can bear no more:
What can the handsome gipsy have in view
In trifling thus, as she appears to do?
I, who for months have labour'd to succeed,
Have only lived her vanity to feed.
"O! you will make me room—'tis very kind,
And meant for him—it tells him he must mind;
Must not be careless:—I can serve to draw
The soldier on, and keep the man in awe.
O! I did think she had a guileless heart,
Without deceit, capriciousness, or art;
And yet a stranger, with a coat of red,
Has, by an hour's attention, turn'd her head.
"Ah! how delicious was the morning-drive,
The soul awaken'd, and its hopes alive;
How dull this scene by trifling minds enjoy'd,
The heart in trouble and its hope destroy'd.
Well, now we land—And will he yet support
This part? What favour has he now to court?
Favour! O, no! He means to quit the fair;
How strange! how cruel! Will she not despair?
Well! take her hand—no further if you please,
I cannot suffer fooleries like these:—
How? 'Love to Julia!' to his wife?—O! dear
And injured creature, how must I appear,
Thus haughty in my looks, and in my words severe?
Her love to Julia, to the school-day friend
To whom those letters she has lately penn'd!
Can she forgive? And now I think again,
The man was neither insolent nor vain;
Good humour chiefly would a stranger trace,
Were he impartial, in the air or face;
And I so splenetic the whole way long,
And she so patient—it was very wrong.

The boat had landed in a shady scene;
The grove was in its glory, fresh and green;
The showers of late had swell'd the branch and bough,
And the sun's fervour made them pleasant now.
Hard by, an oak arose in all its pride,
And threw its arms along the water's side:
Its leafy limbs, that on the glassy lake
Stretch far, and all those dancing shadows make.
And now we walk—now smaller parties seek
Or sun or shade as pleases—Shall I speak?
Shall I forgiveness ask, and then apply
For—O! that vile and intercepting cry!
Alas! what mighty ills can trifles make—
An hat! the idiot's—fallen in the lake!
What serious mischief can such idlers do?
I almost wish the head had fallen too.
No more they leave us, but will hover round,
As if amusement at our cost they found;
Vex'd and unhappy I indeed had been,
Had I not something in my charmer seen
Like discontent, that, though corrected, dwelt
On that dear face, and told me what she felt.
"Now must we cross the lake, and as we cross'd
Was my whole soul in sweet emotion lost;
Clouds in white volumes roll'd beneath the moon,
Softening her light that on the waters shone:
This was such bliss! even then it seem'd relief
To veil the gladness in a show of grief.
We sigh'd as we conversed, and said, how deep
This lake on which those broad dark shadows sleep;
There is between us and a watery grave
But a thin plank, and yet our fate we brave.
'What if it burst?' 'Matilda, then my care
Would be for thee: all danger I would dare,
And, should my efforts fail, thy fortune would I share.'
'The love of life,' she said, 'would powerful prove!'—
'O! not so powerful as the strength of love.'—
A look of kindness gave the grateful maid,
That had the real effort more than paid.
"But here we land, and haply now may choose
Companions home—our way, too, we may lose:
In these drear, dark, inosculating lanes,
The very native of his doubt complains;
No wonder then that in such lonely ways
A stranger, heedless of the country, strays;
A stranger, too, whose many thoughts all meet
In one design, and none regard his feet.
"'Is this the path?' the cautious fair one cries;

I answer, 'Yes!'—'We shall our friends surprise,'
She added, sighing—I return the sighs.
"'Will they not wonder?' 'O! they would, indeed,
Could they the secrets of this bosom read,
These chilling doubts, these trembling hopes I feel!
The faint, fond hopes I can no more conceal—
I love thee, dear Matilda!—to confess
The fact is dangerous, fatal to suppress.
"'And now in terror I approach the home
Where I may wretched but not doubtful come;
Where I must be all ecstasy, or all—
O! what will you a wretch rejected call?
Not man, for I shall lose myself, and be
A creature lost to reason, losing thee.
"'Speak, my Matilda! on the rack of fear
Suspend me not—I would my sentence hear,
Would learn my fate—Good Heaven! and what portend
These tears?—and fall they for thy wretched friend?
Or'—but I cease; I cannot paint the bliss,
From a confession soft and kind as this;
Nor where we walk'd, nor how our friends we met.
Or what their wonder—I am wondering yet;
For he who nothing heeds has nothing to forget.
"All thought, yet thinking nothing—all delight
In every thing, but nothing in my sight!
Nothing I mark or learn, but am possess'd
Of joys I cannot paint, and I am bless'd
In all that I conceive—whatever is, is best.
Ready to aid all beings, I would go
The world around to succour human wo;
Yet am so largely happy, that it seems
There are no woes, and sorrows are but dreams.
"There is a college joy, to scholars known,
When the first honours are proclaim'd their own;
There is ambition's joy, when in their race
A man surpassing rivals gains his place;
There is a beauty's joy, amid a crowd
To have that beauty her first fame allow'd;
And there's the conqueror's joy, when, dubious held
And long the fight, he sees the foe repell'd.
"But what are these, or what are other joys,
That charm kings, conquerors, beauteous nymphs and boys,
Or greater yet, if greater yet be found,
To that delight when love's dear hope is crown'd?
To the first beating of a lover's heart,
When the loved maid endeavours to impart,
Frankly yet faintly, fondly yet in fear,
The kind confession that he holds so dear?

Now in the morn of our return how strange
Was this new feeling, this delicious change;
That sweet delirium, when I gazed in fear,
That all would yet be lost and disappear.
"Such was the blessing that I sought for pain,
In some degree to be myself again;
And when we met a shepherd old and lame,
Cold and diseased, it seem'd my blood to tame;
And I was thankful for the moral sight,
That soberized the vast and wild delight."

TALES OF THE HALL

BOOK VII

THE ELDER BROTHER

Conversation—Story of the elder Brother—His romantic Views and Habits—The Scene of his
Meditations—Their Nature—Interrupted by an Adventure—The Consequences of it—A strong and
permanent Passion—Search of its Object—Long ineffectual—How found—The first Interview—The
second—End of the Adventure—Retirement.

TALES OF THE HALL

BOOK VII

THE ELDER BROTHER

"Thanks, my dear Richard; and, I pray thee, deign
To speak the truth—does all this love remain,
And all this joy? for views and flights sublime,
Ardent and tender, are subdued by time.
Speakst thou of her to whom thou madest thy vows,
Of my fair sister, of thy lawful spouse?
Or art thou talking some frail love about,
The rambling fit, before th' abiding gout?"
Nay, spare me, Brother, an adorer spare:
Love and the gout! thou wouldst not these compare?"
"Yea, and correctly; teasing ere they come,
They then confine their victim to his home:
In both are previous feints and false attacks,
Both place the grieving patient on their racks:

They both are ours, with all they bring, for life,
'Tis not in us t' expel or gout or wife;
On man a kind of dignity they shed,
A sort of gloomy pomp about his bed;
Then, if he leaves them, go where'er he will,
They have a claim upon his body still;
Nay, when they quit him, as they sometimes do,
What is there left t' enjoy or to pursue?—
But dost thou love this woman?"
"O! beyond
What I can tell thee of the true and fond:
Hath she not soothed me, sick, enrich'd me, poor,
And banish'd death and misery from my door?
Has she not cherish'd every moment's bliss,
And made an Eden of a world like this?
When Care would strive with us his watch to keep,
Has she not sung the snarling fiend to sleep?
And when Distress has look'd us in the face,
Has she not told him, 'thou art not Disgrace?'"
"I must behold her, Richard; I must see
This patient spouse who sweetens misery—
But didst thou need, and wouldst thou not apply?—
Nay thou wert right—but then how wrong was I!"
"My indiscretion was—"
"No more repeat;
Would I were nothing worse than indiscreet;—
But still there is a plea that I could bring,
Had I the courage to describe the thing."
"Then, thou too, Brother, couldst of weakness tell;
Thou, too, hast found the wishes that rebel
Against the sovereign reason; at some time
Thou hast been fond, heroic, and sublime;
Wrote verse, it may be, and for one dear maid
The sober purposes of life delay'd;
From year to year the fruitless chase pursued,
And hung enamour'd o'er the flying good.
Then, be thy weakness to a Brother shown,
And give him comfort who displays his own."
"Ungenerous youth! dost thou presuming ask
A man so grave his failings to unmask?
What if I tell thee of a waste of time,
That on my spirit presses as a crime,
Wilt thou despise me?—I, who, soaring, fell
So late to rise—Hear then the tale I tell;
Who tells what thou shalt hear, esteems his hearer well.

"Yes, my dear Richard, thou shalt hear me own
Follies and frailties thou hast never known;

Thine was a frailty,—folly, if you please—
But mine a flight, a madness, a disease.
"Turn with me to my twentieth year, for then
The lover's frenzy ruled the poet's pen;
When virgin reams were soil'd with lays of love,
The flinty hearts of fancied nymphs to move:
Then was I pleased in lonely ways to tread,
And muse on tragic tales of lovers dead;
For all the merit I could then descry
In man or woman was for love to die.
"I mused on charmers chaste, who pledged their truth,
And left no more the once-accepted youth;
Though he disloyal, lost, diseased, became,
The widow'd turtle's was a deathless flame.
This faith, this feeling, gave my soul delight:
Truth in the lady, ardour in the knight.
"I built me castles wondrous rich and rare,
Few castle-builders could with me compare;
The hall, the palace, rose at my command,
And these I fill'd with objects great and grand.
Virtues sublime, that nowhere else would live,
Glory and pomp, that I alone could give;
Trophies and thrones, by matchless valour gain'd,
Faith unreproved, and chastity unstain'd;
With all that soothes the sense and charms the soul,
Came at my call, and were in my control.
"And who was I? a slender youth and tall,
In manner awkward, and with fortune small;
With visage pale; my motions quick and slow,
That fall and rising in the spirits show;
For none could more by outward signs express
What wise men lock within the mind's recess.
Had I a mirror set before my view,
I might have seen what such a form could do;
Had I within the mirror truth beheld,
I should have such presuming thoughts repell'd:
But, awkward as I was, without the grace
That gives new beauty to a form or face,
Still I expected friends most true to prove,
And grateful, tender, warm, assiduous love.
"Assured of this, that love's delicious bond
Would hold me ever faithful, ever fond,
It seem'd but just that I in love should find
A kindred heart as constant and as kind.
Give me, I cried, a beauty: none on earth
Of higher rank or nobler in her birth;
Pride of her race, her father's hope and care,
Yet meek as children of the cottage are;

Nursed in the court, and there by love pursued,
But fond of peace, and blest in solitude;
By rivals honour'd, and by beauties praised,
Yet all unconscious of the envy raised.
Suppose her this, and from attendants freed,
To want my prowess in a time of need,
When safe and grateful she desires to show
She feels the debt that she delights to owe,
And loves the man who saved her in distress—
So fancy will'd, nor would compound for less.
"This was my dream.—In some auspicious hour,
In some sweet solitude, in some green bower,
Whither my fate should lead me, there, unseen,
I should behold my fancy's gracious queen,
Singing sweet song! that I should hear awhile,
Then catch the transient glory of a smile;
Then at her feet with trembling hope should kneel,
Such as rapt saints and raptured lovers feel:
To watch the chaste unfoldings of her heart,
In joy to meet, in agony to part,
And then in tender song to soothe my grief,
And hail, in glorious rhyme, my Lady of the Leaf.
"To dream these dreams I chose a woody scene,
My guardian-shade, the world and me between;
A green inclosure, where beside its bound
A thorny fence beset its beauties round,
Save where some creature's force had made a way
For me to pass, and in my kingdom stray.
Here then I stray'd, then sat me down to call,
Just as I will'd, my shadowy subjects all!
Fruits of all minds conceived on every coast—
Fay, witch, enchanter, devil, demon, ghost;
And thus with knights and nymphs, in halls and bowers,
In war and love, I pass'd unnumber'd hours.
Gross and substantial beings all forgot,
Ideal glories beam'd around the spot,
And all that was, with me, of this poor world was not.
"Yet in this world there was a single scene,
That I allow'd with mine to intervene.
This house, where never yet my feet had stray'd,
I with respect and timid awe survey'd;
With pleasing wonder I have oft-times stood,
To view these turrets rising o'er the wood;
When fancy to the halls and chambers flew,
Large, solemn, silent, that I must not view;
The moat was then, and then o'er all the ground
Tall elms and ancient oaks stretch'd far around;
And where the soil forbad the nobler race,

Dwarf trees and humbler shrubs had found their place,
Forbidding man in their close hold to go,
Haw, gatter, holm, the service and the sloe;
With tangling weeds that at the bottom grew,
And climbers all above their feathery branches threw.
Nor path of man or beast was there espied;
But there the birds of darkness loved to hide,
The loathed toad to lodge, and speckled snake to glide.
"To me this hall, thus view'd in part, appear'd
A mansion vast. I wonder'd, and I fear'd.
There as I wander'd, fancy's forming eye
Could gloomy cells and dungeons dark espy;
Winding through these, I caught th' appalling sound
Of troubled souls, that guilty minds confound,
Where murder made its way, and mischief stalk'd around.
Above the roof were raised the midnight storms,
And the wild lights betray'd the shadowy forms.
"With all these flights and fancies, then so dear,
I reach'd the birth-day of my twentieth year;
And in the evening of a day in June
Was singing—as I sang—some heavenly tune.
My native tone, indeed, was harsh and hoarse,
But he who feels such powers can sing of course—
Is there a good on earth, or gift divine,
That fancy cannot say, behold! 'tis mine?
"So was I singing, when I saw descend
From this old seat a lady and her friend;
Downward they came with steady pace and slow,
Arm link'd in arm, to bless my world below.
I knew not yet if they escaped, or chose
Their own free way; if they had friends or foes—
But near to my dominion drew the pair,
Link'd arm in arm, and walk'd, conversing, there.
"I saw them ere they came, myself unseen,
My lofty fence and thorny bound between—
And one alone, one matchless face I saw,
And, though at distance, felt delight and awe:
Fancy and truth adorn'd her; fancy gave
Much, but not all; truth help'd to make their slave.
For she was lovely, all was not the vain
Or sickly homage of a fever'd brain;
No! she had beauty, such as they admire
Whose hope is earthly, and whose love desire;
Imagination might her aid bestow,
But she had charms that only truth could show.
"Their dress was such as well became the place,
But one superior; hers the air, the grace,
The condescending looks, that spoke the nobler race.

Slender she was and tall; her fairy-feet
Bore her right onward to my shady seat;
And O! I sigh'd that she would nobly dare
To come, nor let her friend th' adventure share;
But see how I in my dominion reign,
And never wish to view the world again.
"Thus was I musing, seeing with my eyes
These objects, with my mind her fantasies,
And chiefly thinking—is this maid, divine
As she appears, to be this queen of mine?
Have   from henceforth beauty in my view,
Not airy all, but tangible and true?
Here then I fix, here bound my vagrant views,
And here devote my heart, my time, my muse.
"She saw not this, though ladies early trace
Their beauty's power, the glories of their face;
Yet knew not this fair creature—could not know
That new-born love that I too soon must show!
And I was musing—how shall I begin?
How make approach my unknown way to win,
And to that heart, as yet untouch'd, make known
The wound, the wish, the weakness of my own?
Such is my part, but—Mercy! what alarm?
Dare aught on earth that sovereign beauty harm?
Again—the shrieking charmers—how they rend
The gentle air—The shriekers lack a friend—
They are my princess and th' attendant maid,
In so much danger, and so much afraid!—
But whence the terror?—Let me haste and see
What has befallen them who cannot flee—
Whence can the peril rise? What can that peril be? }
"It soon appear'd, that while this nymph divine
Moved on, there met her rude uncivil kine,
Who knew her not—the damsel was not there
Who kept them—all obedient—in her care;
Strangers they thus defied and held in scorn,
And stood in threat'ning posture, hoof and horn;
While Susan—pail in hand—could stand the while
And prate with Daniel at a distant stile.
"As feeling prompted, to the place I ran,
Resolved to save the maids and show the man.
Was each a cow like that which challenged Guy,
I had resolved t' attack it, and defy
In mortal combat! to repel or die!
That was no time to parley—or to say,
I will protect you—fly in peace away!
Lo! yonder stile—but with an air of grace,
As I supposed, I pointed to the place.

"The fair ones took me at my sign, and flew,
Each like a dove, and to the stile withdrew;
Where safe, at distance, and from terrors free,
They turn'd to view my beastly foes and me.
"I now had time my business to behold,
And did not like it—let the truth be told:
The cows, though cowards, yet in numbers strong,
Like other mobs, by might defended wrong;
In man's own pathway fix'd, they seem'd disposed
For hostile measure, and in order closed,
Then halted near me, as I judged, to treat,
Before we came to triumph or defeat.
"I was in doubt: 'twas sore disgrace, I knew,
To turn my back, and let the cows pursue;
And should I rashly mortal strife begin,
'Twas all unknown who might the battle win;
And yet to wait, and neither fight nor fly,
Would mirth create—I could not that deny;
It look'd as if for safety I would treat,
Nay, sue for peace—No! rather come defeat!
'Look to me, loveliest of thy sex! and give
One cheering glance, and not a cow shall live;
For lo! this iron bar, this strenuous arm,
And those dear eyes to aid me as a charm.'
"Say, goddess! Victory! say, on man or cow
Meanest thou now to perch?—On neither now—
For, as I ponder'd, on their way appear'd
The Amazonian milker of the herd;
These, at the wonted signals, made a stand,
And woo'd the nymph of the relieving hand;
Nor heeded now the man, who felt relief
Of other kind, and not unmix'd with grief;
For now he neither should his courage prove,
Nor in his dying moments boast his love.
"My sovereign beauty with amazement saw—
So she declared—the horrid things in awe;
Well pleased, she witness'd what respect was paid
By such brute natures—Every cow afraid,
And kept at distance by the powers of one,   }
Who had to her a dangerous service done,
That prudence had declined, that valour's self might shun.
"So thought the maid, who now, beyond the stile,
Received her champion with a gracious smile;
Who now had leisure on those charms to dwell,
That he could never from his thought expel.
There are, I know, to whom a lover seems,
Praising his mistress, to relate his dreams;
But, Richard, looks like those, that angel-face

Could I no more in sister-angel trace;
O! it was more than fancy! it was more
Than in my darling views I saw before,
When I my idol made, and my allegiance swore.
"Henceforth 'twas bliss upon that face to dwell,
Till every trace became indelible;
I bless'd the cause of that alarm, her fright,
And all that gave me favour in her sight,
Who then was kind and grateful, till my mind,
Pleased and exulting, awe awhile resign'd.
For in the moment when she feels afraid,
How kindly speaks the condescending maid;
She sees her danger near, she wants her lover's aid.
As fire electric, when discharged, will strike
All who receive it, and they feel alike,
So in the shock of danger and surprise
Our minds are struck, and mix, and sympathise.
"But danger dies, and distance comes between
My state and that of my all glorious queen;
Yet much was done—upon my mind a chain
Was strongly fix'd, and likely to remain;
Listening, I grew enamour'd of the sound,
And felt to her my very being bound;
I bless'd the scene, nor felt a power to move,
Lost in the ecstacies of infant-love.
"She saw and smiled; the smile delight convey'd,
My love encouraged, and my act repaid.
In that same smile I read the charmer meant
To give her hero chaste encouragement;
It spoke, as plainly as a smile can speak,
'Seek whom you love, love freely whom you seek.'
"Thus, when the lovely witch had wrought her charm,
She took th' attendant maiden by the arm,
And left me fondly gazing, till no more
I could the shade of that dear form explore;
Then to my secret haunt I turn'd again,
Fire in my heart, and fever in my brain;
That face of her for ever in my view,
Whom I was henceforth fated to pursue,
To hope I knew not what—small hope in what I knew.
"O! my dear Richard, what a waste of time
Gave I not thus to lunacy sublime;
What days, months, years, (to useful purpose lost)
Has not this dire infatuation cost?
To this fair vision I, a [bonded] slave,
Time, duty, credit, honour, comfort, gave;
Gave all—and waited for the glorious things
That hope expects, but fortune never brings.

Yet let me own, while I my fault reprove,
There is one blessing still affix'd to love—
To love like mine—for, as my soul it drew
From reason's path, it shunn'd dishonour's too;
It made my taste refined, my feelings nice,
And placed an angel in the way of vice.
"This angel now, whom I no longer view'd,
Far from this scene her destined way pursued;
No more that mansion held a form so fair,
She was away, and beauty was not there.
"Such, my dear Richard, was my early flame,
My youthful frenzy—give it either name;
It was the withering bane of many a year,
That past away in causeless hope and fear—
The hopes, the fears, that every dream could kill,
Or make alive, and lead my passive will.
"At length I learnt one name my angel bore,
And Rosabella I must now adore:
Yet knew but this—and not the favour'd place
That held the angel or th' angelic race;
Nor where, admired, the sweet enchantress dwelt,
But I had lost her—that, indeed, I felt.
"Yet, would I say, she will at length be mine!
Did ever hero hope or love resign?
Though men oppose, and fortune bids despair,
She will in time her mischief well repair,
And I, at last, shall wed this fairest of the fair!
"My thrifty uncle, now return'd, began
To stir within me what remain'd of man;
My powerful frenzy painted to the life,
And ask'd me if I took a dream to wife?
Debate ensued, and, though not well content,
Upon a visit to his house I went.
He, the most saving of mankind, had still
Some kindred feeling; he would guide my will,
And teach me wisdom—so affection wrought,
That he to save me from destruction sought:
To him destruction, the most awful curse
Of misery's children, was—an empty purse!
He his own books approved, and thought the pen
An useful instrument for trading men;
But judged a quill was never to be slit
Except to make it for a merchant fit.
He, when inform'd how men of taste could write,
Look'd on his ledger with supreme delight;
Then would he laugh, and, with insulting joy,
Tell me aloud, 'that's poetry, my boy;
These are your golden numbers—them repeat,

The more you have, the more you'll find them sweet—
Their numbers move all hearts—no matter for their feet.
Sir, when a man composes in this style,
What is to him a critic's frown or smile?
What is the puppy's censure or applause
To the good man who on his banker draws,
Buys an estate, and writes upon the grounds,
'Pay to A. B. an hundred thousand pounds?'
Thus, my dear nephew, thus your talents prove;
Leave verse to poets, and the poor to love.'
"Some months I suffered thus, compell'd to sit
And hear a wealthy kinsman aim at wit;
Yet there was something in his nature good,
And he had feeling for the tie of blood.
So, while I languish'd for my absent maid
I some observance to my uncle paid."
"Had you inquired?" said Richard.
"I had placed
Inquirers round, but nothing could be traced;
Of every reasoning creature at this Hall,
And tenant near it, I applied to all—
'Tell me if she'—and I described her well—
'Dwelt long a guest, or where retired to dwell?'
But no! such lady they remember'd not—
They saw that face, strange beings! and forgot.
Nor was inquiry all; but I pursued
My soul's first wish, with hope's vast strength endued:
I cross'd the seas, I went where strangers go,
And gazed on crowds as one who dreads a foe,
Or seeks a friend; and, when I sought in vain,
Fled to fresh crowds, and hoped, and gazed again."
"It was a strong possession"—"Strong and strange,
I felt the evil, yet desired not change.
Years now had flown, nor was the passion cured,
But hope had life, and so was life endured;
The mind's disease, with all its strength, stole on,
Till youth, and health, and all but love were gone.
And there were seasons, Richard, horrid hours
Of mental suffering! they o'erthrew my powers,
And made my mind unsteady—I have still,
At times, a feeling of that nameless ill,
That is not madness—I could always tell
My mind was wandering—knew it was not well;
Felt all my loss of time, the shameful waste
Of talents perish'd, and of parts disgraced.
But though my mind was sane, there was a void—
My understanding seem'd in part destroy'd;
I thought I was not of my species one,

But unconnected, injured and undone!
"While in this state, once more my uncle pray'd
That I would hear—I heard, and I obey'd;
For I was thankful that a being broke
On this my sadness, or an interest took
In my poor life—but, at his mansion, rest
Came with its halcyon stillness to my breast.
Slowly there enter'd in my mind concern
For things about me—I would something learn,
And to my uncle listen; who, with joy,
Found that ev'n yet I could my powers employ,
Till I could feel new hopes my mind possess,
Of ease at least, if not of happiness;
Till, not contented, not in discontent,
As my good uncle counsell'd, on I went;
Conscious of youth's great error—nay, the crime
Of manhood now—a dreary waste of time!
Conscious of that account which I must give
How life had past with me—I strove to live.
"Had I, like others, my first hope attain'd,
I must, at least, a certainty have gain'd;
Had I, like others, lost the hope of youth,
Another hope had promised greater truth;
But I in baseless hopes, and groundless views,
Was fated time, and peace, and health to lose,
Impell'd to seek, for ever doom'd to fail,
Is—I distress you—let me end my tale.
"Something one day occurr'd about a bill
That was not drawn with true mercantile skill,
And I was ask'd and authorized to go
To seek the firm of Clutterbuck and Co.;
Their hour was past—but when I urged the case,
There was a youth who named a second place;
Where, on occasions of important kind,
I might the man of occupation find
In his retirement, where he found repose
From the vexations that in business rose.
I found, though not with ease, this private seat
Of soothing quiet, wisdom's still retreat.
"The house was good, but not so pure and clean
As I had houses of retirement seen;
Yet men, I knew, of meditation deep,
Love not their maidens should their studies sweep;
His room I saw, and must acknowledge, there
Were not the signs of cleanliness or care:
A female servant, void of female grace,
Loose in attire, proceeded to the place;
She stared intrusive on my slender frame,

And boldly ask'd my business and my name.
"I gave them both; and, left to be amused,
Well as I might, the parlour I perused.
The shutters half unclosed, the curtains fell
Half down, and rested on the window-sill,
And thus, confusedly, made the room half visible.
Late as it was, the little parlour bore
Some tell-tale tokens of the night before;
There were strange sights and scents about the room,
Of food high-season'd, and of strong perfume;
Two unmatch'd sofas ample rents display'd;
Carpet and curtains were alike decay'd;
A large old mirror, with once-gilded frame,
Reflected prints that I forbear to name,
Such as a youth might purchase—but, in truth,
Not a sedate or sober-minded youth;
The cinders yet were sleeping in the grate,
Warm from the fire, continued large and late,
As left by careless folk in their neglected state;
The chairs in haste seem'd whirl'd about the room,
As when the sons of riot hurry home,
And leave the troubled place to solitude and gloom.
"All this, for I had ample time, I saw,
And prudence question'd—should we not withdraw?
For he who makes me thus on business wait,
Is not for business in a proper state;
But man there was not, was not he for whom
To this convenient lodging I was come;
No! but a lady's voice was heard to call
On my attention—and she had it all;
For lo! she enters, speaking ere in sight,
'Monsieur! I shall not want the chair to-night—
Where shall I see him?—This dear hour atones
For all affection's hopeless sighs and groans'—
Then, turning to me—'Art thou come at last?
A thousand welcomes—be forgot the past;
Forgotten all the grief that absence brings,
Fear that torments, and jealousy that stings—
All that's cold, injurious, and unkind,
Be it for ever banish'd from the mind;
And in that mind, and in that heart be now
The soft endearment, and the binding vow!'
"She spoke—and o'er the practised features threw
The looks that reason charm, and strength subdue.
"Will you not ask, how I beheld that face,
Or read that mind, and read it in that place?
I have tried, Richard, oft-times, and in vain,
To trace my thoughts, and to review their train—

If train there were—that meadow, grove, and stile;
The fright, th' escape, her sweetness and her smile;
Years since elapsed, and hope, from year to year,
To find her free—and then to find her here!
"But is it she?—O! yes; the rose is dead;
All beauty, fragrance, freshness, glory fled;
But yet 'tis she—the same and not the same—
Who to my bower an heavenly being came;
Who waked my soul's first thought of real bliss;
Whom long I sought; and now I find her—this.
"I cannot paint her—something I had seen
So pale and slim, and tawdry and unclean;
With haggard looks, of vice and wo the prey,
Laughing in langour, miserably gay.
Her face, where face appear'd, was amply spread,
By art's coarse pencil, with ill-chosen red,
The flower's fictitious bloom, the blushing of the dead;
But still the features were the same, and strange
My view of both—the sameness and the change,
That fix'd me gazing and my eye enchain'd,
Although so little of herself remain'd;
It is the creature whom I loved, and yet
Is far unlike her—Would I could forget
The angel or her fall! the once adored
Or now despised! the worshipp'd or deplored!
"'O! Rosabella!' I prepared to say,
'Whom I have loved,' but prudence whisper'd nay,
And folly grew ashamed—discretion had her day.
She gave her hand; which, as I lightly press'd,
The cold but ardent grasp my soul oppress'd;
The ruin'd girl disturb'd me, and my eyes
Look'd, I conceive, both sorrow and surprise.
"I spoke my business—'He,' she answer'd, 'comes
And lodges here—he has the backward rooms—
He now is absent, and I chanced to hear
Will not before to-morrow eve appear,
And may be longer absent—O! the night
When you preserved me in that horrid fright;
A thousand, thousand times, asleep, awake,
I thought of what you ventured for my sake—
Now, have you thought—yet tell me so—deceive
Your Rosabella, willing to believe!
O! there is something in love's first-born pain
Sweeter than bliss—it never comes again—
But has your heart been faithful?'—Here my pride,
To anger rising, her attempt defied—
'My faith must childish in your sight appear,
Who have been faithful—to how many, dear?'

"If words had fail'd, a look explain'd their style,
She could not blush assent, but she could smile.
Good heaven! I thought, have I rejected fame,
Credit, and wealth, for one who smiles at shame?
"She saw me thoughtful—saw it, as I guess'd,
With some concern, though nothing she express'd.
"'Come, my dear friend, discard that look of care,
All things were made to be, as all things are;
All to seek pleasure as the end design'd,
The only good in matter or in mind;
So was I taught by one, who gave me all
That my experienced heart can wisdom call.
"'I saw thee young, love's soft obedient slave,
And many a sigh to my young lover gave;
And I had, spite of cowardice or cow,
Return'd thy passion, and exchanged my vow;
But, while I thought to bait the amorous hook,
One set for me my eager fancy took;
There was a crafty eye, that far could see,
And through my failings fascinated me:
Mine was a childish wish, to please my boy;
His a design, his wishes to enjoy.
O! we have both about the world been tost,
Thy gain I know not—I, they cry, am lost;
So let the wise ones talk; they talk in vain,
And are mistaken both in loss and gain;
'Tis gain to get whatever life affords,
'Tis loss to spend our time in empty words.
"'I was a girl, and thou a boy wert then,
Nor aught of women knew, nor I of men;
But I have traffick'd in the world, and thou,
Doubtless, canst boast of thy experience now;
Let us the knowledge we have gain'd produce,
And kindly turn it to our common use.'
"Thus spoke the siren in voluptuous style,
While I stood gazing and perplex'd the while,
Chain'd by that voice, confounded by that smile.
And then she sang, and changed from grave to gay,
Till all reproach and anger died away.

"'&My Damon was the first to wake
The gentle flame that cannot die;
My Damon is the last to take
The faithful bosom's softest sigh:
The life between is nothing worth,
O! cast it from thy thought away;
Think of the day that gave it birth,
And this its sweet returning day.

"'Buried be all that has been done,
Or say that naught is done amiss;
For who the dangerous path can shun
In such bewildering world as this?
But love can every fault forgive,
Or with a tender look reprove;
And now let naught in memory live,
But that we meet, and that we love.'"

"And then she moved my pity; for she wept,
And told her miseries till resentment slept;
For when she saw she could not reason blind,
She pour'd her heart's whole sorrows on my mind,
With features graven on my soul, with sighs
Seen but not heard, with soft imploring eyes,
And voice that needed not, but had the aid
Of powerful words to soften and persuade.
O! I repent me of the past; and sure
Grief and repentance make the bosom pure;
Yet meet thee not with clean and single heart,
As on the day we met—and but to part!
Ere I had drank the cup that to my lip
Was held, and press'd till I was forced to sip.
I drank indeed, but never ceased to hate—
It poison'd, but could not intoxicate.
T' excuse my fall I plead not love's excess,
But a weak orphan's need and loneliness.
I had no parent upon earth—no door
Was oped to me—young, innocent, and poor,
Vain, tender, and resentful—and my friend,
Jealous of one who must on her depend,
Making life misery—You could witness then
That I was precious in the eyes of men;
So, made by them a goddess, and denied
Respect and notice by the women's pride;
Here scorn'd, there worshipp'd—will it strange appear,
Allured and driven, that I settled here?
Yet loved it not; and never have I pass'd
One day, and wish'd another like the last.
There was a fallen angel, I have read,
For whom their tears the sister-angels shed,
Because, although she ventured to rebel,
She was not minded like a child of hell.—
Such is my lot! and will it not be given
To grief like mine, that I may think of heaven;
Behold how there the glorious creatures shine,
And all my soul to grief and hope resign?'"

"I wonder'd, doubting—and, is this a fact,
I thought, or part thou art disposed to act?
"'Is it not written, He, who came to save
Sinners, the sins of deepest dye forgave;
That he his mercy to the sufferers dealt,
And pardon'd error when the ill was felt?
Yes! I would hope, there is an eye that reads
What s within, and sees the heart that bleeds—
But who on earth will one so lost deplore,
And who will help that lost one to restore?
'Who will on trust the sigh of grief receive;
And—all things warring with belief—believe?'
"Soften'd, I said—'Be mine the hand and heart,
If with your world you will consent to part.'
She would—she tried—Alas! she did not know
How deeply rooted evil habits grow:
She felt the truth upon her spirits press,
But wanted ease, indulgence, show, excess,
Voluptuous banquets, pleasures—not refined,
But such as soothe to sleep th' opposing mind—
She look'd for idle vice, the time to kill,
And subtle, strong apologies for ill;
And thus her yielding, unresisting soul
Sank, and let sin confuse her and control:
Pleasures that brought disgust yet brought relief,
And minds she hated help'd to war with grief."
"Thus then she perish'd?"—
"Nay—but thus she proved
Slave to the vices that she never loved;
But, while she thus her better thoughts opposed,
And woo'd the world, the world's deceptions closed.—
I had long lost her; but I sought in vain   7
To banish pity—still she gave me pain;
Still I desired to aid her—to direct,
And wish'd the world, that won her, to reject;
Nor wish'd in vain—there came, at length, request
That I would see a wretch with grief oppress'd,
By guilt affrighted—and I went to trace
Once more the vice-worn features of that face,
That sir-wreck'd being! and I saw her laid
Where never worldly joy a visit paid,
That world receding fast! the world to come
Conceal'd in terror, ignorance, and gloom,
Sins, sorrow, and neglect: with not a spark
Of vital hope—all horrible and dark—
It frighten'd me!—I thought, and shall not I
Thus feel? thus fear?—this danger can I fly?
Do I so wisely live that I can calmly die?

"The wants I saw I could supply with ease,
But there were wants of other kind than these;
Th' awakening thought, the hope-inspiring view—
The doctrines awful, grand, alarming, true—
Most painful to the soul, and yet most healing too.
Still, I could something offer, and could send
For other aid—a more important friend,
Whose duty call'd him, and his love no less,
To help the grieving spirit in distress;
To save in that sad hour the drooping prey,
And from its victim drive despair away.
All decent comfort[s] round the sick were seen;
The female helpers quiet, sober, clean;
Her kind physician with a smile appear'd,
And zealous love the pious friend endear'd;
While I, with mix'd sensations, could inquire,
'Hast thou one wish, one unfulfill'd desire?
Speak every thought, nor unindulged depart,
If I can make thee happier than thou art.'
"Yes! there was yet a female friend, an old
And grieving nurse! to whom it should be told—
I would tell—that she, her child, had fail'd,
And turn'd from truth! yet truth at length prevail'd.
"'Twas in that chamber, Richard, I began
To think more deeply of the end of man:
Was it to jostle all his fellows by,
To run before them, and say, 'here am I,
Fall down, and worship?'—Was it, life throughout,
With circumspection keen to hunt about,
As spaniels for their game, where might be found
Abundance more for coffers that abound?
Or was it life's enjoyments to prefer,
Like this poor girl, and then to die like her?
No! He, who gave the faculties, design'd
Another use for the immortal mind:
There is a state in which it will appear
With all the good and ill contracted here;
With gain and loss, improvement and defect;
And then, my soul! what hast thou to expect
For talents laid aside, life's waste, and time's neglect?
"Still as I went came other change—the frame
And features wasted, and yet slowly came
The end; and so inaudible the breath,
And still the breathing, we exclaim'd—"tis death!'
But death it was not: when, indeed, she died,
I sat and his last gentle stroke espied:
When—as it came—or did my fancy trace
That lively, lovely flushing o'er the face,

Bringing back all that my young heart impress'd?
It came—and went!—She sigh'd, and was at rest!
"Adieu, I said, fair Frailty! dearly cost
The love I bore thee—time and treasure lost;
And I have suffer'd many years in vain;
Now let me something in my sorrows gain:
Heaven would not all this wo for man intend
If man's existence with his we should end;
Heaven would not pain, and grief, and anguish give,
If man was not by discipline to live;
And for that brighter, better world prepare,
That souls with souls, when purified, shall share,
Those stains all done away that must not enter there.
"Home I return'd, with spirits in that state
Of vacant wo I strive not to relate;
Nor how, deprived of all her hope and strength,
My soul turn'd feebly to the world at length.
I travell'd then till health again resumed
Its former seat—I must not say re-bloom'd;
And then I fill'd, not loth, that favourite place
That has enrich'd some seniors of our race;
Patient and dull I grew; my uncle's praise
Was largely dealt me on my better days;
A love of money—other love at rest—
Came creeping on, and settled in my breast;
The force of habit held me to the oar,
Till I could relish what I scorn'd before:
I now could talk and scheme with men of sense,
Who deal for millions, and who sigh for pence;
And grew so like them, that I heard with joy
Old Blueskin said I was a pretty boy;
For I possess'd the caution, with the zeal,
That all true lovers of their interest feel.
Exalted praise! and to the creature due
Who loves that interest solely to pursue
"But I was sick, and sickness brought disgust;
My peace I could not to my profits trust:
Again some views of brighter kind appear'd,
My heart was humbled, and my mind was clear'd;
I felt those helps that souls diseased restore,
And that cold frenzy, avarice, raged no more.
From dreams of boundless wealth I then arose;   }
This place, the scene of infant bliss, I chose;   }
And here I find relief, and here I seek repose.   }
"Yet much is lost, and not yet much is found,
But what remains, I would believe, is sound:
That first wild passion, that last mean desire,
Are felt no more; but holier hopes require

A mind prepared and steady—my reform
Has fears like his, who, suffering in a storm,
Is on a rich but unknown country cast,
The future fearing, while he feels the past;
But whose more cheerful mind, with hope imbued,
Sees through receding clouds the rising good."

TALES OF THE HALL

BOOK VIII

THE SISTER

Morning Walk and Conversation—Visit at a Cottage—Characters of the Sisters—Lucy and Jane—Their
Lovers—Their Friend the Banker and his Lady—Their Intimacy—Its Consequence—Different Conduct of
the Lovers—The Effect upon the Sisters—Their present State—The Influence of their Fortune upon the
Minds of either.

TALES OF THE HALL

BOOK VIII

THE SISTERS

The morning shone in cloudless beauty bright;
Richard his letters read with much delight;
George from his pillow rose in happy tone,
His bosom's lord sat lightly on his throne.
They read the morning news—they saw the sky
Inviting call'd them, and the earth was dry.
"The day invites us, brother," said the 'squire;
"Come, and I'll show thee something to admire:
We still may beauty in our prospects trace;
If not, we have them in both mind and face.
"'Tis but two miles—to let such women live
Unseen of him, what reason can I give?
Why should not Richard to the girls be known?
Would I have all their friendship for my own?—
Brother, there dwell, yon northern hill below,
Two favourite maidens, whom 'tis good to know;
Young, but experienced; dwellers in a cot,
Where they sustain and dignify their lot;

The best good girls in all our world below—
O! you must know them—Come! and you shall know.
"But lo! the morning wastes—here, Jacob, stir—
If Phœbe comes, do you attend to her;
And let not Mary get a chattering press
Of idle girls to hear of her distress.
Ask her to wait till my return—and hide
From her meek mind your plenty and your pride;
Nor vex a creature, humble, sad, and still,
By your coarse bounty, and your rude good-will."
This said, the brothers hasten'd on their way,
With all the foretaste of a pleasant day.
The morning purpose in the mind had fix'd
The leading thought, and that with others mix'd.
"How well it is," said George, "when we possess
The strength that bears us up in our distress;
And need not the resources of our pride,
Our fall from greatness and our wants to hide;
But have the spirit and the wish to show,
We know our wants as well as others know.
'Tis true, the rapid turns of fortune's wheel
Make even the virtuous and the humble feel:
They for a time must suffer, and but few
Can bear their sorrows and our pity too.
"Hence all these small expedients, day by day,
Are used to hide the evils they betray:
When, if our pity chances to be seen,
The wounded pride retorts, with anger keen,
And man's insulted grief takes refuge in his spleen.
"When Timon's board contains a single dish,
Timon talks much of market-men and fish,
Forgetful servants, and th' infernal cook,
Who always spoil'd whate'er she undertook.
"But say it tries us from our height to fall,
Yet is not life itself a trial all?
And not a virtue in the bosom lives,
That gives such ready pay as patience gives;
That pure submission to the ruling mind,
Fix'd, but not forced; obedient, but not blind,
The will of heaven to make her own she tries,
Or makes her own to heaven a sacrifice.
"And is there aught on earth so rich or rare,
Whose pleasures may with virtue's pains compare?
This fruit of patience, this the pure delight
That 'tis a trial in her Judge's sight;
Her part still striving duty to sustain,
Not spurning pleasure, not defying pain;
Never in triumph till her race be won,

And never fainting till her work be done."
With thoughts like these they reach'd the village brook,
And saw a lady sitting with her book;
And so engaged she heard not, till the men
Were at her side, nor was she frighten'd then;
But to her friend, the 'squire, his smile return'd,
Through which the latent sadness he discern'd.
The stranger-brother at the cottage door
Was now admitted, and was strange no more;
Then of an absent sister he was told,
Whom they were not at present to behold;
Something was said of nerves, and that disease,
Whose varying powers on mind and body seize,
Enfeebling both!—Here chose they to remain
One hour in peace, and then return'd again.
"I know not why," said Richard, "but I feel
The warmest pity on my bosom steal
For that dear maid! How well her looks express
For this world's good a cherish'd hopelessness!
A resignation that is so entire,
It feels not now the stirrings of desire;
What now to her is all the world esteems?
She is awake, and cares not for its dreams;
But moves while yet on earth, as one above
Its hopes and fears—it[s] loathing and its love.
"But shall I learn," said he, "these sisters' fate?"—
And found his brother willing to relate.

"The girls were orphans early; yet I saw,
When young, their father—his profession law;
He left them but a competence, a store
That made his daughters neither rich nor poor;
Not rich, compared with some who dwelt around;
Not poor, for want they neither fear'd nor found;
Their guardian uncle was both kind and just,
One whom a parent might in dying trust;
Who, in their youth, the trusted store improved,
And, when he ceased to guide them, fondly loved.
"These sister beauties were in fact the grace
Of yon small town,—it was their native place;
Like Saul's famed daughters were the lovely twain,
As Micah, Lucy, and as Merab, Jane:
For this was tall, with free commanding air,
And that was mild, and delicate, and fair.
"Jane had an arch delusive smile, that charm'd
And threaten'd too; alluring, it alarm'd;
The smile of Lucy her approval told,
Cheerful, not changing; neither kind nor cold.

"When children, Lucy love alone possess'd,
Jane was more punished and was more caress'd;
If told the childish wishes, one bespoke
A lamb, a bird, a garden, and a brook;
The other wish'd a joy unknown, a rout
Or crowded ball, and to be first led out.
"Lucy loved all that grew upon the ground,
And loveliness in all things living found;
The gilded fly, the fern upon the wall,
Were nature's works, and admirable all;
Pleased with indulgence of so cheap a kind,
Its cheapness never discomposed her mind.
"Jane had no liking for such things as these,
Things pleasing her must her superiors please;
The costly flower was precious in her eyes,
That skill can vary, or that money buys;
Her taste was good, but she was still afraid,
Till fashion sanction'd the remarks she made.
"The sisters read, and Jane with some delight,
The satires keen that fear or rage excite,
That men in power attack, and ladies high,
And give broad hints that we may know them by.
She was amused when sent to haunted rooms,
Or some dark passage where the spirit comes
Of one once murder'd! then she laughing read,
And felt at once the folly and the dread.
As rustic girls to crafty gipsies fly,
And trust the liar though they fear the lie,
Or as a patient, urged by grievous pains,
Will fee the daring quack whom he disdains:
So Jane was pleased to see the beckoning hand,
And trust the magic of the Ratcliffe-wand.
"In her religion—for her mind, though light,
Was not disposed our better views to slight—
Her favourite authors were a solemn kind,
Who fill with dark mysterious thoughts the mind;
And who with such conceits her fancy plied,
Became her friend, philosopher, and guide.
"She made the Progress of the Pilgrim one
To build a thousand pleasant views upon;
All that connects us with a world above
She loved to fancy, and she long'd to prove;
Well would the poet please her, who could lead
Her fancy forth, yet keep untouch'd her creed.
"Led by an early custom, Lucy spied,
When she awaked, the Bible at her side;
That, ere she ventured on a world of care,
She might for trials, joys or pains prepare,

For every dart a shield, a guard for every snare.
"She read not much of high heroic deeds,
Where man the measure of man's power exceeds;
But gave to luckless love and fate severe
Her tenderest pity and her softest tear.
"She mix'd not faith with fable, but she trod
Right onward, cautious in the ways of God;
Nor did she dare to launch on seas unknown,
In search of truths by some adventurers shown,
But her own compass used, and kept a course her own.
"The maidens both their loyalty declared,
And in the glory of their country shared;
But Jane that glory felt with proud delight,
When England's foes were vanquish'd in the fight;
While Lucy's feelings for the brave who bled
Put all such glorious triumphs from her head.
"They both were frugal; Lucy from the fear
Of wasting that which want esteems so dear,
But finds so scarce, her sister from the pain
That springs from want, when treated with disdain.
"Jane borrow'd maxims from a doubting school,
And took for truth the test of ridicule;
Lucy saw no such virtue in a jest:
Truth was with her of ridicule a test.
"They loved each other with the warmth of youth,
With ardour, candour, tenderness, and truth;
And, though their pleasures were not just the same,
Yet both were pleased whenever one became;
Nay, each would rather in the act rejoice,
That was th' adopted, not the native choice.
"Each had a friend, and friends to minds so fond
And good are soon united in the bond;
Each had a lover; but it seem'd that fate
Decreed that these should not approximate.
Now Lucy's lover was a prudent swain,
And thought, in all things, what would be his gain;
The younger sister first engaged his view,
But with her beauty he her spirit knew;
Her face he much admired, 'but, put the case,'
Said he, 'I marry, what is then a face?
At first it pleases to have drawn the lot;
He then forgets it, but his wife does not;
Jane too,' he judged, 'would be reserved and nice,
And many lovers had enhanced her price.'
"Thus thinking much, but hiding what he thought,
The prudent lover Lucy's favour sought,
And he succeeded—she was free from art,
And his appear'd a gentle guileless heart;

Such she respected; true, her sister found
His placid face too ruddy and too round,
Too cold and inexpressive; such a face
Where you could nothing mark'd or manly trace.
"But Lucy found him to his mother kind,
And saw the Christian meekness of his mind;
His voice was soft, his temper mild and sweet,
His mind was easy, and his person neat.
"Jane said he wanted courage; Lucy drew
No ill from that, though she believed it too;
'It is religious, Jane, be not severe;'
'Well, Lucy, then it is religious fear,'
Nor could the sister, great as was her love,
A man so lifeless and so cool approve.
"Jane had a lover, whom a lady's pride
Might wish to see attending at her side,
Young, handsome, sprightly, and with good address,
Not mark'd for folly, error or excess;
Yet not entirely from their censure free
Who judge our failings with severity.
The very care he took to keep his name
Stainless, with some was evidence of shame.
"Jane heard of this, and she replied, 'Enough;
Prove out the facts, and I resist not proof;
Nor is my heart so easy as to love
The man my judgment bids me not approve.'
But yet that heart a secret joy confess'd,
To find no slander on the youth would rest;
His was, in fact, such conduct, that a maid
Might think of marriage, and be not afraid;
And she was pleased to find a spirit high,
Free from all fear, that spurn'd hypocrisy.
"'What fears my sister?' said the partial fair,
For Lucy fear'd,—'Why tell me to beware?
No smooth deceitful varnish can I find;
His is a spirit generous, free, and kind;
And all his flaws are seen, all floating in his mind.
A little boldness in his speech. What then?
It is the failing of these generous men.
A little vanity, but—O! my dear,
They all would show it, were they all sincere.
"'But come, agreed; we'll lend each other eyes
To see our favourites, when they wear disguise;
And all those errors that will then be shown
Uninfluenced by the workings of our own.'
"Thus lived the sisters, far from power removed,
And far from need, both loving and beloved.
Thus grew, as myrtles grow; I grieve at heart

That I have pain and sorrow to impart.
But so it is, the sweetest herbs that grow
In the lone vale, where sweetest waters flow,
Ere drops the blossom, or appears the fruit,
Feel the vile grub, and perish at the root;
And, in a quick and premature decay,
Breathe the pure fragrance of their life away.
"A town was near, in which the buildings all
Were large, but one pre-eminently tall—
An huge high house. Without there was an air
Of lavish cost; no littleness was there;
But room for servants, horses, whiskies, gigs,
And walls for pines and peaches, grapes and figs;
Bright on the sloping glass the sunbeams shone,
And brought the summer of all climates on.
"Here wealth its prowess to the eye display'd,
And here advanced the seasons, there delay'd;
Bid the due heat each growing sweet refine,
Made the sun's light with grosser fire combine,
And to the Tropic gave the vigour of the Line.
"Yet, in the master of this wealth behold
A light vain coxcomb taken from his gold,
Whose busy brain was weak, whose boasting heart was cold.
O! how he talk'd to that believing town,
That he would give it riches and renown;
Cause a canal where treasures were to swim,
And they should owe their opulence to him!
In fact, of riches he insured a crop,
So they would give him but a seed to drop.
As used the alchymist his boasts to make,
'I give you millions for the mite I take:'
The mite they never could again behold,
The millions all were Eldorado gold.
"By this professing man the country round
Was search'd to see where money could be found.
"The thriven farmer, who had lived to spare,
Became an object of especial care;
He took the frugal tradesman by the hand,
And wish'd him joy of what he might command;
And the industrious servant, who had laid
His saving by, it was his joy to aid;
Large talk, and hints of some productive plan
Half named, won all his hearers to a man;
Uncertain projects drew them wondering on,
And avarice listen'd till distrust was gone.
But when to these dear girls he found his way,
All easy, artless, innocent were they;
When he compelled his foolish wife to be

At once so great, so humble, and so free;
Whom others sought, nor always with success!
But they were both her pride and happiness;
And she esteem'd them, but attended still
To the vile purpose of her husband's will;
And, when she fix'd his snares about their mind,
Respected those whom she essay'd to blind;
Nay with esteem she some compassion gave
To the fair victims whom she would not save.
"The Banker's wealth and kindness were her themes,
His generous plans, his patriotic schemes;
What he had done for some, a favourite few,
What for his favourites still he meant to do;
Not that he always listen'd—which was hard—
To her, when speaking of her great regard
For certain friends—'but you, as I may say,
Are his own choice—I am not jealous—nay!'
"Then came the man himself, and came with speed,
As just from business of importance freed;
Or just escaping, came with looks of fire,
As if he'd just attain'd his full desire;
As if Prosperity and he for life
Were wed, and he was showing off his wife;
Pleased to display his influence, and to prove
Himself the object of her partial love;
Perhaps with this was join'd the latent fear,
The time would come when he should not be dear.
"Jane laugh'd at all their visits and parade,
And call'd it friendship in an hot-house made;
A style of friendship suited to his taste,
Brought on, and ripen'd, like his grapes, in haste;
She saw the wants that wealth in vain would hide,
And all the tricks and littleness of pride;
On all the wealth would creep the vulgar stain,
And grandeur strove to look itself in vain.
"Lucy perceived—but she replied, 'why heed
Such small defects?—they're very kind indeed!'
And kind they were, and ready to produce
Their easy friendship, ever fit for use,
Friendship that enters into all affairs,
And daily wants, and daily gets, repairs.
"Hence at the cottage of the sisters stood
The Banker's steed—he was so very good;
Oft through the roads, in weather foul or fair,
Their friend's gay carriage bore the gentle pair;
His grapes and nectarines woo'd the virgins' hand;
His books and roses were at their command,
And costly flowers—he took upon him shame

That he could purchase what he could not name.
"Lucy was vex'd to have such favours shown,
And they returning nothing of their own;
Jane smiled, and begg'd her sister to believe,—
'We give at least as much as we receive.'
"Alas! and more; they gave their ears and eyes,
His splendor oft-times took them by surprise;
And, if in Jane appear'd a meaning smile,
She gazed, admired, and paid respect the while;
Would she had rested there! Deluded maid,
She saw not yet the fatal price she paid;
Saw not that wealth, though join'd with folly, grew
In her regard; she smiled, but listened too;
Nay would be grateful, she would trust her all,
Her funded source—to him a matter small;
Taken for their sole use, and ever at their call,
To be improved—he knew not how indeed,
But he had methods—and they must succeed.
"This was so good, that Jane, in very pride,
To spare him trouble, for a while denied;
And Lucy's prudence, though it was alarm'd,
Was by the splendor of the Banker charm'd;
What was her paltry thousand pounds to him,
Who would expend five thousand on a whim?
And then the portion of his wife was known;
But not that she reserved it for her own.
"Lucy her lover trusted with the fact,
And frankly ask'd, 'if he approved the act?'
'It promised well,' he said; 'he could not tell
How it might end, but sure it promised well;
He had himself a trifle in the Bank,
And should be sore uneasy if it sank.'
"Jane from her lover had no wish to hide
Her deed; but was withheld by maiden pride;
To talk so early—as if one were sure
Of being his; she could not that endure.
"But when the sisters were apart, and when
They freely spoke of their affairs and men,
They thought with pleasure of the sum improved,
And so presented to the men they loved.
"Things now proceeded in a quiet train;
No cause appear'd to murmur or complain;
The monied man, his ever-smiling dame,
And their young darlings, in their carriage came.
Jane's sprightly lover smiled their pomp to see,
And ate their grapes, with gratitude and glee;
But with the freedom there was nothing mean,
Humble, or forward, in his freedom seen;

His was the frankness of a mind that shows
It knows itself, nor fears for what it knows.
But Lucy's ever humble friend was awed
By the profusion he could not applaud;
He seem'd indeed reluctant to partake
Of the collation that he could not make;
And this was pleasant in the maiden's view,—
Was modesty—was moderation too;
Though Jane esteem'd it meanness; and she saw
Fear in that prudence, avarice in that awe.
"But both the lovers now to town are gone;
By business one is call'd, by duty one;
While rumour rises—whether false or true
The ladies knew not—it was known to few—
But fear there was, and on their guardian-friend
They for advice and comfort would depend
When rose the day; meantime from Belmont-place
Came vile report, predicting quick disgrace.
"'Twas told—the servants, who had met to thank
Their lord for placing money in his Bank—
Their kind free master, who such wages gave,
And then increased whatever they could save—
They who had heard they should their savings lose,
Were weeping, swearing, drinking at the news;
And still the more they drank, the more they wept,
And swore, and rail'd, and threatened, till they slept
"The morning truth confirm'd the evening dread;
The Bank was broken, and the Banker fled;
But left a promise that his friends should have,
To the last shilling—what his fortunes gave.
"The evil tidings reach'd the sister-pair,
And one like Sorrow look'd, and one Despair;
They from each other turn'd th' afflicting look,
And loth and late the painful silence broke.
"'The odious villain!' Jane in wrath began;
In pity Lucy, 'the unhappy man!
When time and reason our affliction heal,
How will the author of our sufferings feel?'
"'And let him feel, my sister—let the woes
That he creates be bane to his repose!
Let them be felt in his expiring hour,
When death brings all his dread, and sin its power:
Then let the busy foe of mortals state
The pangs he caused, his own to aggravate!
"'Wretch! when our life was glad, our prospers gay,
With savage hand to sweep them all away!
And he must know it—know when he beguiled
His easy victims—how the villain smiled!

"'Oh! my dear Lucy, could I see him crave
The food denied, a beggar and a slave,
To stony hearts he should with tears apply,
And Pity's self withhold the struggling sigh;
Or, if relenting weakness should extend
Th' extorted scrap that justice would not lend,
Let it be poison'd by the curses deep
Of every wretch whom he compels to weep!'
"'Nay, my sweet sister, if you thought such pain
Were his, your pity would awake again;
Your generous heart the wretch's grief would feel,
And you would soothe the pangs you could not heal.'
"'Oh! never, never,—I would still contrive
To keep the slave whom I abhorr'd alive;
His tortured mind with horrid fears to fill,
Disturb his reason, and misguide his will;
Heap coals of fire, to lie like melted lead,
Heavy and hot, on his accursed head;
Not coals that mercy kindles hearts to melt,
But he should feel them hot as fires are felt,
Corroding ever, and through life the same,
Strong self-contempt and ever-burning shame;
Let him so wretched live that he may fly
To desperate thoughts, and be resolved to die—
And then let death such frightful visions give,
That he may dread th' attempt, and beg to live!'
So spake th' indignant maid, when Lucy sigh'd,
And, waiting softer times, no more replied.
"Barlow was then in town; and there he thought
Of bliss to come, and bargains to be bought;
And was returning homeward—when he found
The Bank was broken, and his venture drown'd.
"'Ah! foolish maid,' he cried, 'and what wilt thou
Say for thy friends and their excesses now?
All now is brought completely to an end;
What can the spendthrift now afford to spend?
Had my advice been—true, I gave consent,
The thing was purposed; what could I prevent?
"'Who will her idle taste for flowers supply—
Who send her grapes and peaches? let her try;—
There's none will give her, and she cannot buy.
"'Yet would she not be grateful if she knew
What to my faith and generous love was due?
Daily to see the man who took her hand,
When she had not a sixpence at command;
Could I be sure that such a quiet mind
Would be for ever grateful, mild, and kind,
I might comply—but how will Bloomer act,

'When he becomes acquainted with the fact?
The loss to him is trifling—but the fall
From independence, that to her is all;
Now, should he marry, 'twill be shame to me
To hold myself from my engagement free;
And should he not, it will be double grace
To stand alone in such a trying case.
"'Come then, my Lucy, to thy faithful heart
And humble love I will my views impart;
Will see the grateful tear that softly steals
Down the fair face and all thy joy reveals;
And when I say it is a blow severe,
Then will I add—restrain, my love, the tear,
And take this heart, so faithful and so fond,
Still bound to thine; and fear not for that bond.'
"He said; and went, with purpose he believed
Of generous nature—so is man deceived.
"Lucy determined that her lover's eye
Should not distress nor supplication spy;
That in her manner he should nothing find
To indicate the weakness of her mind.
He saw no eye that wept, no frame that shook;
No fond appeal was made by word or look;
Kindness there was, but join'd with some restraint;
And traces of the late event were faint.
"He look'd for grief deploring, but perceives
No outward token that she longer grieves;
He had expected for his efforts praise,
For he resolved the drooping mind to raise;
She would, he judged, be humble, and afraid
That he might blame her rashness and upbraid;
And lo! he finds her in a quiet state,
Her spirit easy and her air sedate:
As if her loss was not a cause for pain,
As if assured that he would make it gain,—
"Silent awhile, he told the morning news,
And what he judged they might expect to lose;
He thought himself, whatever some might boast,
The composition would be small at most,
Some shabby matter; she would see no more
The tithe of what she held in hand before.
"How did her sister feel? and did she think
Bloomer was honest, and would never shrink?
'But why that smile; is loss like yours so light
That it can aught like merriment excite?
Well, he is rich, we know, and can afford
To please his fancy, and to keep his word;
To him 'tis nothing; had he now a fear,

He must the meanest of his sex appear;
But the true honour, as I judge the case,
Is both to feel the evil and embrace.'
"Here Barlow stopp'd, a little vex'd to see
No fear or hope, no dread or ecstasy.
Calmly she spoke—'Your prospects, sir, and mine
Are not the same—their union I decline;
Could I believe the hand for which you strove
Had yet its value, did you truly love,
I had with thanks addressed you, and replied,
Wait till your feelings and my own subside,
Watch your affections, and, if still they live,
What pride denies, my gratitude shall give.'
Ev'n then, in yielding, I had first believed
That I conferr'd the favour, not received.
"'You I release—nay, hear me—I impart
Joy to your soul—I judge not of your heart.
Think'st thou a being, to whom God has lent
A feeling mind, will have her bosom rent
By man's reproaches? Sorrow will be thine,
For all thy pity prompts thee to resign!
Think'st thou that meekness' self would condescend
To take the husband when she scorns the friend?
Forgive the frankness, and rejoice for life
Thou art not burden'd with so poor a wife.
"'Go! and be happy—tell, for the applause
Of hearts like thine, we parted, and the cause
Give, as it pleases.' With a foolish look
That a dull school-boy fixes on his book
That he resigns, with mingled shame and joy,
So Barlow went, confounded like the boy.
"Jane, while she wept to think her sister's pain
Was thus increased, felt infinite disdain;
Bound as she was, and wedded by the ties
Of love and hope, that care and craft despise,
She could but wonder that a man, whose taste
And zeal for money had a Jew disgraced,
Should love her sister; yet with this surprise,
She felt a little exultation rise;
Hers was a lover who had always held
This man as base, by generous scorn impell'd,
And yet, as one, of whom for Lucy's sake
He would a civil distant notice take.
"Lucy, with sadden'd heart and temper mild,
Bow'd to correction, like an humbled child,
Who feels the parent's kindness, and who knows
Such the correction he who loves bestows.
"Attending always, but attending more

When sorrow ask'd his presence than before,
Tender and ardent, with the kindest air
Came Bloomer, fortune's error to repair;
Words sweetly soothing spoke the happy youth,
With all the tender earnestness of truth.
"There was no doubt of his intention now—
He will his purpose with his love avow;
So judged the maid; yet, waiting, she admired
His still delaying what he most desired;
Till, from her spirit's agitation free,
She might determine when the day should be.
With such facility the partial mind
Can the best motives for its favourites find.
"Of this he spake not, but he stayed beyond
His usual hour—attentive still and fond;—
The hand yet firmer to the hand he prest,
And the eye rested where it loved to rest;
Then took he certain freedoms, yet so small
That it was prudish so the things to call;
Things they were not—'Describe'—that none can do,
They had been nothing had they not been new;
It was the manner and the look; a maid,
Afraid of such, is foolishly afraid;
For what could she explain? The piercing eye
Of jealous fear could nought amiss descry.
"But some concern now rose; the youth would seek
Jane by herself, and then would nothing speak,
Before not spoken; there was still delay,
Vexatious, wearying, wasting, day by day.
"'He does not surely trifle!' Heaven forbid!
She now should doubly scorn him if he did.
"Ah! more than this, unlucky girl! is thine;
Thou must the fondest views of life resign;
And in the very time resign them too,
When they were brightening on the eager view.
I will be brief,—nor have I heart to dwell
On crimes they almost share who paint them well.
"There was a moment's softness, and it seem'd
Discretion slept, or so the lover dream'd;
And, watching long the now confiding maid,
He thought her guardless, and grew less afraid;
Led to the theme that he had shunn'd before,
He used a language he must use no more—
For if it answers, there is no more need,
And no more trial, should it not succeed.
"Then made he that attempt, in which to fail
Is shameful,—still more shameful to prevail.
"Then was there lightning in that eye that shed

Its beams upon him—and his frenzy fled;
Abject and trembling at her feet he laid,
Despised and scorn'd by the indignant maid,
Whose spirits in their agitation rose,
Him, and her own weak pity, to oppose:
As liquid silver in the tube mounts high,
Then shakes and settles as the storm goes by.
"While yet the lover stay'd, the maid was strong,
But when he fled, she droop'd and felt the wrong—
Felt the alarming chill, the enfeebled breath,
Closed the quick eye, and sank in transient death.
So Lucy found her; and then first that breast
Knew anger's power, and own'd the stranger guest.
"'And is this love? Ungenerous! Has he too
Been mean and abject? Is no being true?'
For Lucy judged that, like her prudent swain,
Bloomer had talk'd of what a man might gain;
She did not think a man on earth was found,
A wounded bosom, while it bleeds, to wound;
Thought not that mortal could be so unjust,
As to deprive affliction of its trust;
Thought not a lover could the hope enjoy,
That must the peace he should promote destroy;
Thought not, in fact, that in the world were those,
Who to their tenderest friends are worse than foes,
Who win the heart, deprive it of its care,
Then plant remorse and desolation there.
"Ah! cruel he, who can that heart deprive
Of all that keeps its energy alive;
Can see consign'd to shame the trusting fair,
And turn confiding fondness to despair;
To watch that time—a name is not assign'd
For crime so odious, nor shall learning find.
Now, from that day has Lucy laid aside
Her proper cares, to be her sister's guide,
Guard, and protector. At their uncle's farm
They past the period of their first alarm,
But soon retired, nor was he grieved to learn
They made their own affairs their own concern.
"I knew not then their worth; and, had I known,
Could not the kindness of a friend have shown;
For men they dreaded; they a dwelling sought,
And there the children of the village taught;
There, firm and patient, Lucy still depends
Upon her efforts, not upon her friends;
She is with persevering strength endued,
And can be cheerful—for she will be good.
"Jane too will strive the daily tasks to share,

That so employment may contend with care;
Not power, but will, she shows, and looks about
On her small people, who come in and out;
And seems of what they need, or she can do, in doubt.
"There sits the chubby crew on seats around,
While she, all rueful at the sight and sound,
Shrinks from the free approaches of the tribe,
Whom she attempts, lamenting to describe;
With stains the idlers gather'd in their way,
The simple stains of mud, and mould, and clay,
And compound of the streets, of what we dare not say;
With hair uncomb'd, grimed face, and piteous look,
Each heavy student takes the odious book,
And on the lady casts a glance of fear,
Who draws the garment close as he comes near;
She then for Lucy's mild forbearance tries,
And from her pupils turns her brilliant eyes,
Making new efforts, and with some success,
To pay attention while the students guess;
Who to the gentler mistress fain would glide,
And dread their station at the lady's side.
"Such is their fate;—there is a friendly few
Whom they receive, and there is chance for you;
Their school, and something gather'd from the wreck
Of that bad Bank, keeps poverty in check;
And true respect, and high regard, are theirs,
The children's profit, and the [parents'] prayers.
"With Lucy rests the one peculiar care,
That few must see, and none with her may share;
More dear than hope can be, more sweet than pleasures are.
For her sad sister needs the care of love
That will direct her, that will not reprove,
But waits to warn: for Jane will walk alone,
Will sing in low and melancholy tone;
Will read or write, or to her plants will run,
To shun her friends,—alas! her thoughts to shun.
"It is not love alone disturbs her rest,
But loss of all that ever hope possess'd:
Friends ever kind, life's lively pleasures, ease,
When her enjoyments could no longer please;
These were her comforts then! she has no more of these.
"Wrapt in such thoughts, she feels her mind astray,
But knows 'tis true that she has lost her way;
For Lucy's smile will check the sudden flight,
And one kind look let in the wonted light.
"Fits of long silence she endures, then talks
Too much—with too much ardour, as she walks;
But still the shrubs that she admires dispense

Their balmy freshness to the hurried sense,
And she will watch their progress, and attend
Her flowering favourites as a guardian friend;
To sun or shade she will her sweets remove,
'And here,' she says, 'I may with safety love.'
"But there are hours when on that bosom steals
A rising terror—then indeed she feels—
Feels how she loved the promised good, and how
She feels the failure of the promise now.
"'That other spoiler did as robbers do,
Made poor our state, but not disgraceful too,
This spoiler shames me, and I look within
To find some cause that drew him on to sin;
He and the wretch who could thy worth forsake
Are the fork'd adder and the loathsome snake;
Thy snake could slip in villain-fear away,
But had no fang to fasten on his prey.
"'Oh! my dear Lucy, I had thought to live
With all the comforts easy fortunes give;
A wife caressing, and caress'd—a friend,
Whom he would guide, advise, consult, defend,
And make his equal;—then I fondly thought
Among superior creatures to be brought;
And, while with them, delighted to behold
No eye averted, and no bosom cold;—
Then at my home, a mother, to embrace
My—Oh! my sister, it was surely base!
I might forget the wrong; I cannot the disgrace.
"'Oh! when I saw that triumph in his eyes,
I felt my spirits with his own arise;
I call'd it joy, and said, the generous youth
Laughs at my loss—no trial for his truth,
It is a trifle he can not lament,
A sum but equal to his annual rent;
And yet that loss, the cause of every ill,
Has made me poor, and him—'
"'O! poorer still;
Poorer, my Jane, and far below thee now:
The injurer he,—the injured sufferer thou;
And shall such loss afflict thee?'—
"'Lose I not
With him what fortune could in life allot?
Lose I not hope, life's cordial, and the views
Of an aspiring spirit?—O! I lose
Whate'er the happy feel, whatever the sanguine choose.
"'Would I could lose this bitter sense of wrong,
And sleep in peace—but it will not be long!
And here is something, Lucy, in my brain—

I know not what—it is a cure for pain;
But is not death!—no beckoning hand I see,
No voice I hear that comes alone to me;
It is not death, but change; I am not now
As I was once—nor can I tell you how;
Nor is it madness—ask, and you shall find
In my replies the soundness of my mind:
O! I should be a trouble all day long;
A very torment, if my head were wrong.'
"At times there is upon her features seen
What moves suspicion—she is too serene.
Such is the motion of a drunken man,
Who steps sedately, just to show he can.
Absent at times she will her mother call,
And cry at mid-day, 'then good night to all.'
But most she thinks there will some good ensue
From something done, or what she is to do;
Long wrapt in silence, she will then assume
An air of business, and shake off her gloom;
Then cry exulting, 'O! it must succeed,
There are ten thousand readers—all men read:
There are my writings—you shall never spend
Your precious moments to so poor an end;
Our [peasants'] children may be taught by those
Who have no powers such wonders to compose;
So let me call them—what the world allows,
Surely a poet without shame avows;
Come, let us count what numbers we believe
Will buy our work—Ah! sister, do you grieve?
You weep; there's something I have said amiss,
And vex'd my sister—What a world is this!
And how I wander!—Where has fancy run?
Is there no poem? Have I nothing done?
Forgive me, Lucy, I had fix'd my eye,
And so my mind, on works that cannot die,
Marmion and Lara yonder in the case;
And so I put me in the poet's place.
"'Still, be not frighten'd; it is but a dream
I am not lost, bewilder'd though I seem;
I will obey thee—but suppress thy fear—
I am at ease—then why that silly tear?'
"Jane, as these melancholy fits invade
The busy fancy, seeks the deepest shade;
She walks in ceaseless hurry, till her mind
Will short repose in verse and music find;
Then her own songs to some soft tune she sings,
And laughs, and calls them melancholy things;
Not frenzy all; in some her erring Muse

Will sad, afflicting, tender strains infuse;
Sometimes on death she will her lines compose,
Or give her serious page of solemn prose;
And still those favourite plants her fancy please,
And give to care and anguish rest and ease.

"'Let me not have this gloomy view,
About my room, around my bed;
But morning roses, wet with dew,
To cool my burning brows instead.
As flow'rs that once in Eden grew,
Let them their fragrant spirits shed,
And every day the sweets renew,
Till I, a fading flower, am dead.

"'Oh! let the herbs I loved to rear
Give to my sense their perfumed breath;
Let them be placed about my bier,
And grace the gloomy house of death.
I'll have my grave beneath an hill,
Where, only Lucy's self shall know;

"'Where runs the pure pellucid rill
Upon its gravelly bed below;
There violets on the borders blow,
And insects their soft light display,
Till, as the morning sunbeams glow,
The cold phosphoric fires decay.

"'That is the grave to Lucy shown,
The soil a pure and silver sand;
The green cold moss above it grown,
Unpluck'd of all but maiden hand:
In virgin earth, till then unturn'd,
There let my maiden form be laid,
Nor let my changed clay be spurn'd,
Nor for new guest that bed be made.

"'There will the lark, the lamb, in sport,
In air, on earth, securely play,
And Lucy to my grave resort,
As innocent, but not so gay.
I will not have the churchyard ground,
With bones all black and ugly grown,
To press my shivering body round,
Or on my wasted limbs be thrown.

"'With ribs and skulls I will not sleep,

In clammy beds of cold blue clay,
Through which the ringed earth-worms creep,
And on the shrouded bosom prey;
I will not have the bell proclaim
When those sad marriage rites begin,
And boys, without regard or shame,
Press the vile mouldering masses in.

"'Say not, it is beneath my care;
I cannot these cold truths allow;
These thoughts may not afflict me there,
But, O! they vex and tease me now,
Raise not a turf, nor set a stone,
That man a maiden's grave may trace;
But thou, my Lucy, come alone,
And let affection find the place.

"'O! take me from a world I hate—
Men cruel, selfish, sensual, cold;
And, in some pure and blessed state,
Let me my sister minds behold:
From gross and sordid views refined,
Our heaven of spotless love to share,
For only generous souls design'd,
And not a man to meet us there.'"

TALES OF THE HALL

BOOK IX

THE PRECEPTOR HUSBAND

The Morning Ride—Conversation—Character of one whom they meet- His early Habits and Mode of
Thinking—The Wife whom he would choose—The one chosen—His Attempts to teach—In History—In
Botany—The Lady's Proficiency—His Complaint—Her Defence and Triumph—The Trial ends.

TALES OF THE HALL

BOOK IX

THE PRECEPTOR HUSBAND

"Whom pass'd we musing near the woodman's shed,
Whose horse not only carried him but led,
That his grave rider might have slept the time,
Or solved a problem, or composed a rhyme?
A more abstracted man within my view
Has never come—He recollected you."
"Yes—he was thoughtful—thinks the whole day long,
Deeply, and chiefly that he once thought wrong;
He thought a strong and kindred mind to trace
In the soft outlines of a trifler's face.
"Poor Finch! I knew him when at school—a boy
Who might be said his labours to enjoy;
So young a pedant that he always took
The girl to dance who most admired her book;
And would the butler and the cook surprise,
Who listen'd to his Latin exercise;
The matron's self the praise of Finch avow'd,
He was so serious, and he read so loud.
But yet, with all this folly and conceit,
The lines he wrote were elegant and neat;
And early promise in his mind appear'd
Of noble efforts when by reason clear'd.
"And when he spoke of wives, the boy would say,
His should be skill'd in Greek and algebra;
For who would talk with one to whom his themes,
And favourite studies, were no more than dreams?
For this, though courteous, gentle, and humane,
The boys contemn'd and hated him as vain,
Stiff and pedantic.—"
"Did the man enjoy,
In after life, the visions of the boy?"—
"At least they form'd his wishes, they were yet
The favourite views on which his mind was set:
He quaintly said, how happy must they prove,
Who, loving, study—or who, studious, love;
Who feel their minds with sciences imbued,
And their warm hearts by beauty's force subdued.
"His widow'd mother, who the world had seen,
And better judge of either sex had been,
Told him that, just as their affairs were placed,
In some respects he must forego his taste;
That every beauty, both of form and mind,
Must be by him, if unendow'd, resign'd;
That wealth was wanted for their joint affairs;
His sisters' portions, and the Hall's repairs.
"The son assented—and the wife must bring
Wealth, learning, beauty, ere he gave the ring;
But as these merits, when they all unite,

Are not produced in every soil and site;
And when produced are not the certain gain
Of him who would these precious things obtain;
Our patient student waited many a year,
Nor saw this phœnix in his walks appear.
But, as views mended in the joint estate,
He would a something in his points abate;
Give him but learning, beauty, temper, sense,
And he would then the happy state commence.
The mother sigh'd, but she at last agreed;
And now the son was likely to succeed.
Wealth is substantial good the fates allot:
We know we have it, or we have it not;
But all those graces which men highly rate
Their minds themselves imagine and create;
And therefore Finch was in a way to find
A good that much depended on his mind.
"He lock'd around, observing, till he saw
Augusta Dallas! when he felt an awe
Of so much beauty and commanding grace,
That well became the honours of her race.
"This lady never boasted of the trash
That commerce brings: she never spoke of cash;
The gentle blood that ran in every vein
At all such notions blush'd in pure disdain.—
"Wealth once relinquished, there was all beside,
As Finch believed, that could adorn a bride;
He could not gaze upon the form and air,
Without concluding all was right and fair;
Her mild but dignified reserve supprest
All free inquiry—but his mind could rest,
Assured that all was well, and in that view was blest.
"And now he asked, 'am I the happy man
Who can deserve her? is there one who can?'
His mother told him, he possess'd the land
That puts a man in heart to ask a hand;
All who possess it feel they bear about
A spell that puts a speedy end to doubt;
But Finch was modest—'May it then be thought
That she can so be gained?'—'She may be sought.—'
'Can love with land be won?'—'By land is beauty bought.
Do not, dear Charles, with indignation glow,
All value that the want of which they know;
Nor do I blame her; none that worth denies;
But can my son be sure of what he buys?
Beauty she has, but with it can you find
The inquiring spirit, or the studious mind?
This wilt thou need who art to thinking prone,

And minds unpair'd had better think alone;
Then how unhappy will the husband be,
Whose sole associate spoils his company?'
This he would try; but all such trials prove
Too mighty for a man disposed to love;
He whom the magic of a face enchains
But little knowledge of the mind obtains;
If by his tender heart the man is led,
He finds how erring is the soundest head.
"The lady saw his purpose; she could meet
The man's inquiry, and his aim defeat;
She had a studied flattery in her look;
She could be seen retiring with a book;
She by attending to his speech could prove
That she for learning had a fervent love—
Yet love alone, she modestly declared;
She must be spared inquiry, and was spared;
Of her poor studies she was not so weak
As in his presence, or at all, to speak;
But to discourse with him who, all agreed,
[Had] read so much, would be absurd indeed;
Ask what he might, she was so much a dunce
She would confess her ignorance at once.
"All this the man believed not—doom'd to grieve
For this belief, he this would not believe:
No! he was quite in raptures to discern
That love, and that avidity to learn.
'Could she have found,' she said, 'a friend, a guide,
Like him, to study had been all her pride;
But, doom'd so long to frivolous employ,
How could she those superior views enjoy?
The day might come—a happy day for her,
When she might choose the ways she should prefer.'
"Then too he learn'd in accidental way,
How much she grieved to lose the given day
In dissipation wild, in visitation gay.
Happy, most happy, must the woman prove
Who proudly looks on him she vows to love;
Who can her humble acquisitions state,
That he will praise, at least will tolerate.
"Still the cool mother sundry doubts express'd,—
'How! is Augusta graver than the rest?
There are three others: they are not inclined
To feed with precious food the empty mind;
Whence this strong relish?' 'It is very strong,'
Replied the son, 'and has possess'd her long;
Increased indeed, I may presume, by views—
We may suppose—ah! may she not refuse?'

'Fear not!—I see the question must be tried,
Nay, is determined—let us to your bride.'
"They soon were wedded, and the nymph appear'd
By all her promised excellence endear'd:
Her words were kind, were cautious, and were few,
And she was proud—of what her husband knew.
"Weeks pass'd away, some five or six, before,
Bless'd in the present, Finch could think of more.
A month was next upon a journey spent,
When to the Lakes the fond companions went;
Then the gay town received them, and, at last,
Home to their mansion, man and wife, they pass'd.
"And now in quiet way they came to live
On what their fortune, love, and hopes would give.
The honied moon had nought but silver rays,
And shone benignly on their early days;
The second moon a light less vivid shed,
And now the silver rays were tinged with lead.
They now began to look beyond the Hall,
And think what friends would make a morning-call;
Their former appetites return'd, and now
Both could their wishes and their tastes avow;
'Twas now no longer 'just what you approve,'
But 'let the wild fowl be to-day, my love.'
In fact the senses, drawn aside by force
Of a strong passion, sought their usual course.
"Now to her music would the wife repair,
To which he listen'd once with eager air;
When there was so much harmony within,
That any note was sure its way to win;
But now the sweet melodious tones were sent
From the struck chords, and none cared where they went.
Full well we know that many a favourite air
That charms a party fails to charm a pair;
And as Augusta play'd she look'd around,
To see if one was dying at the sound;
But all were gone—a husband, wrapt in gloom,
Stalk'd careless, listless, up and down the room.
"And now 'tis time to fill that ductile mind
With knowledge, from his stores of various kind.
His mother, in a peevish mood, had ask'd,
'Does your Augusta profit? is she task'd?'
"'Madam!' he cried, offended with her looks,
'There's time for all things, and not all for books:
Just on one's marriage to sit down, and prate
On points of learning, is a thing I hate.—'
"'Tis right, my son, and it appears to me,
If deep your hatred, you must well agree.'

"Finch was too angry for a man so wise,
And said, 'Insinuation I despise!
Nor do I wish to have a mind so full
Of learned trash—it makes a woman dull:
Let it suffice, that I in her discern
An aptitude, and a desire to learn.—'
"The matron smiled, but she observed a frown
On her son's brow, and calmly sat her down,
Leaving the truth to Time, who solves our doubt,
By bringing his all-glorious daughter out—
Truth! for whose beauty all their love profess;
And yet how many think it ugliness!
"'Augusta, love,' said Finch, 'while you engage
In that embroidery, let me read a page.
Suppose it Hume's; indeed he takes a side,
But still an author need not be our guide;
And, as he writes with elegance and ease,
Do now attend—he will be sure to please.
Here at the Revolution we commence—
We date, you know, our liberties from hence.'
"'Yes, sure,' Augusta answer'd with a smile;
'Our teacher always talk'd about his style,
When we about the Revolution read,
And how the martyrs to the flames were led:
The good old bishops, I forget their names,
But they were all committed to the flames;
Maidens and widows, bachelors and wives—
The very babes and sucklings lost their lives.
I read it all in Guthrie at the school—
What now!—I know you took me for a fool;
There were five bishops taken from the stall,
And twenty widows, I remember all;
And by this token, that our teacher tried
'To cry for pity, till she howl'd and cried.'
"'True, true, my love, but you mistake the thing—
The Revolution that made William king
Is what I mean; the Reformation you,
In Edward and Elizabeth.'—"Tis true;
But the nice reading is the love between
The brave Lord Essex and the cruel queen;
And how he sent the ring to save his head,
Which the false lady kept till he was dead.
"'That is all true; now read, and I'll attend;
But was not she a most deceitful friend?
It was a monstrous, vile, and treacherous thing
To show no pity, and to keep the ring;
But the queen shook her in her dying bed,
And 'God forgive you!' was the word she said;

'Not I for certain;'—Come, I will attend;
So read the Revolutions to an end.'
"Finch, with a timid, strange, inquiring look,
Softly and slowly laid aside the book
With sigh inaudible—'Come, never heed,'
Said he, recovering; 'now I cannot read.'
"They walk'd at leisure through their wood and groves,
In fields and lanes, and talk'd of plants and loves,
And loves of plants.—Said Finch, 'Augusta, dear,
You said you loved to learn,—were you sincere?
Do you remember that you told me once
How much you grieved, and said you were a dunce?
That is, you wanted information. Say,
What would you learn? I will direct your way.'
"'Goodness!' said she, 'what meanings you discern
In a few words! I said I wish'd to learn,
And so I think I did; and you replied,
The wish was good: what would you now beside?
Did not you say it show'd an ardent mind;
And pray what more do you expect to find?'
"'My dear Augusta, could you wish indeed
For any knowledge, and not then proceed?
That is not wishing—'
"'Mercy! how you tease!
You knew I said it with a view to please;
A compliment to you, and quite enough—
You would not kill me with that puzzling stuff!
Sure I might say I wish'd; but that is still
Far from a promise: it is not,—'I will.'
"'But come, to show you that I will not hide
My proper talents, you shall be my guide;
And lady Boothby, when we meet, shall cry,
She's quite as good a botanist as I.'
"'Right, my Augusta;' and, in manner grave,
Finch his first lecture on the science gave;
An introduction—and he said, 'My dear,
Your thought was happy—let us persevere;
And let no trifling cause our work retard.'
Agreed the lady, but she fear'd it hard.
"Now o'er the grounds they rambled many a mile;
He show'd the flowers, the stamina, the style,
Calix and corol, pericarp and fruit,
And all the plant produces, branch and root;
Of these he treated, every varying shape,
Till poor Augusta panted to escape.
He show'd the various foliage plants produce,
Lunate and lyrate, runcinate, retuse;
Long were the learned words, and urged with force.

Panduriform, pinnatifid, premorse,
Latent, and patent, papulous, and plane—
'Oh!' said the pupil, 'it will turn my brain.'
'Fear not,' he answer'd, and again, intent
To fill that mind, o'er class and order went;
And stopping, 'Now,' said he, 'my love, attend.'
'I do,' said she, 'but when will be an end?'—
'When we have made some progress—now begin,
Which is the stigma, show me with the pin;
Come, I have told you, dearest, let me see,
Times very many—tell it now to me.'
"'Stigma! I know,—the things with yellow heads,
That shed the dust, and grow upon the threads;
You call them wives and husbands, but you know
That is a joke—here, look, and I will show
All I remember.'—Doleful was the look
Of the preceptor, when he shut his book—
The system brought to aid them in their view,
And now with sighs return'd—'It will not do.'
"A handsome face first led him to suppose,
There must be talent with such looks as those;
The want of talent taught him now to find
The face less handsome with so poor a mind;
And half the beauty faded, when he found
His cherish'd hopes were falling to the ground.
"Finch lost his spirit; but e'en then he sought
For fancied powers: she might in time be taught.
Sure there was nothing in that mind to fear;
The favourite study did not yet appear.—
"Once he express'd a doubt if she could look
For five succeeding minutes on a book;
When, with awaken'd spirit, she replied,
'He was mistaken, and she would be tried.'
"With this delighted, he new hopes express'd—
'How do I know?—She may abide the test?
Men I have known, and famous in their day,
Who were by chance directed in their way.
I have been hasty.—Well, Augusta, well,
What is your favourite reading? prithee tell;
Our different tastes may different books require—
Yours I may not peruse, and yet admire:
Do then explain.'—'Good Heaven!' said she, in haste,
'How do I hate these lectures upon taste!'
"'I lecture not, my love; but do declare—
You read, you say—what your attainments are.'
"'Oh! you believe,' said she, 'that other things
Are read as well as histories of kings,
And loves of plants, with all that simple stuff

About their sex, of which I know enough.
Well, if I must, I will my studies name,
Blame if you please—I know you love to blame.
When all our childish books were set apart,
The first I read was 'Wanderings of the Heart:'
It was a story, where was done a deed
So dreadful, that alone I fear'd to read.
"'The next was 'The Confessions of a Nun—'
'Twas quite a shame such evil should be done;
'Nun of—no matter for the creature's name,
For there are girls no nunnery can tame.
Then was the story of the Haunted Hall,
Where the huge picture nodded from the wall
When the old lord look'd up with trembling dread,
And I grew pale, and shudder'd as I read.
Then came the tales of Winters, Summers, Springs,
At Bath and Brighton,—they were pretty things!
No ghosts nor spectres there were heard or seen,
But all was love and flight to Gretna-green.
Perhaps your greater learning may despise
What others like, and there your wisdom lies—
Well! do not frown—I read the tender tales
Of lonely cots, retreats in silent vales
For maids forsaken, and suspected wives,
Against whose peace some foe his plot contrives;
With all the hidden schemes that none can clear
Till the last book, and then the ghosts appear.
"'I read all plays that on the boards succeed,
And all the works that ladies ever read—
Shakspeare, and all the rest—I did, indeed,—
Ay! you may stare; but, sir, believe it true
That we can read and learn, as well as you.
"'I would not boast,—but I could act a scene
In any play, before I was fifteen.
"'Nor is this all; for many are the times
I read in Pope and Milton, prose and rhymes;
They were our lessons, and, at ten years old,
I could repeat—but now enough is told.
Sir, I can tell you I my mind applied
To all my studies, and was not denied
Praise for my progress—Are you satisfied?'
"'Entirely, madam! else were I possess'd
By a strong spirit who could never rest.
Yes! yes, no more I question—here I close
The theme for ever—let us to repose.'"

A Friend arrives at the Hall—Old Bachelors and Maids—Relation of one—His Parents—The first Courtship—The second—The third—Long Interval—Travel—Decline of Life—The fourth Lady—Conclusion.

TALES OF THE HALL

BOOK X

THE OLD BACHELOR

Save their kind friend the rector, Richard yet
Had not a favourite of his brother met;
Now at the Hall that welcome guest appear'd,
By trust, by trials, and by time endear'd;
Of him the grateful 'squire his love profess'd,
And full regard—he was of friends the best;
"Yet not to him alone this good I owe,
This social pleasure that our friends bestow;
The sex that wrought in earlier life my woes,
With loss of time who murder'd my repose,
They to my joys administer, nor vex
Me more; and now I venerate the sex;
And boast the friendship of a spinster kind,
Cheerful and pleasant, to her fate resign'd;
Then by her side my bachelor I place,
And hold them honours to the human race.
Yet these are they in tale and song display'd,
The peevish man, and the repining maid;
Creatures made up of misery and spite,
Who taste no pleasures, except those they blight;
From whom th' affrighten'd niece and nephew fly—
Fear'd while they live, and useless till they die.
"Not such these friends of mine; they never meant
That youth should so be lost, or life be spent.
They had warm passions, tender hopes, desires
That youth indulges, and that love inspires;
But fortune frown'd on their designs, displaced
The views of hope, and love's gay dreams disgraced;
Took from the soul her sunny views, and spread

A cloud of dark but varying gloom instead.
And shall we these with ridicule pursue.
Because they did not what they could not do?
If they their lot preferr'd, still why the jest
On those who took the way they judged the best?
But if they sought a change, and sought in vain,
'Tis worse than brutal to deride their pain—
But you will see them; see the man I praise,
The kind protector in my troubled days,
Himself in trouble; you shall see him now,
And learn his worth! and my applause allow."
This friend appear'd, with talents form'd to please,
And with some looks of sprightliness and ease;
To him indeed the ills of life were known,
But misery had not made him all her own.
They spoke on various themes, and George design'd
To show his brother this, the favourite mind;
To lead the friend, by subjects he could choose,
To paint himself, his life, and earlier views,
What he was bless'd to hope, what he was doom'd to lose.
They spoke of marriage, and he understood
Their call on him, and said, "It is not good
To be alone, although alone to be
Is freedom; so are men in deserts free;
Men who unyoked and unattended groan,
Condemn'd and grieved to walk their way alone.
Whatever ills a married pair betide,
Each feels a stay, a comfort, or a guide;
'Not always comfort,' will our wits reply.—
Wits are not judges, nor the cause shall try.
"Have I not seen, when grief his visits paid,
That they were easier by communion made?
True, with the quiet times and days serene,
There have been flying clouds of care and spleen;
But is not man, the solitary, sick
Of his existence, sad and splenetic?
And who will help him, when such evils come,
To bear the pressure or to clear the gloom?
"Do you not find, that joy within the breast
Of the unwedded man is soon suppress'd
While, to the bosom of a wife convey'd,
Increase is by participation made?—
The lighted lamp that gives another light,
Say, is it by th' imparted blaze less bright?
Are not both gainers when the heart's distress
Is so divided that the pain is less?
And when the tear has stood in either eye.
Love's sun shines out, and they are quickly dry."

He ended here—but would he not confess,
How came these feelings on his mind to press?
He would! nor fear'd his weakness to display
To men like them; their weakness too had they.
Bright shone the fire, wine sparkled, sordid care
Was banish'd far, at least appear'd not there;
A kind and social spirit each possess'd,
And thus began his tale the friendly guest.

"Near to my father's mansion—but apart,
I must acknowledge, from my father's heart—
Dwelt a keen sportsman, in a pleasant seat;
Nor met the neighbours as should neighbours meet.
To them revenge appear'd a kind of right,
A lawful pleasure, an avow'd delight;
Their neighbours too blew up their passion's fire,
And urged the anger of each rival-squire;
More still their waspish tempers to inflame,
A party-spirit, friend of anger, came.
Oft would my father cry, 'that tory-knave,
That villain-placeman, would the land enslave.'
Not that his neighbour had indeed a place,
But would accept one—that was his disgrace;
Who, in his turn, was sure my father plann'd
To revolutionize his native land.
He dared the most destructive things advance,
And even pray'd for liberty to France;
Had still good hope that Heaven would grant his prayer,
That he might see a revolution there.
At this the tory-squire was much perplex'd,
'Freedom in France!—what will he utter next?
Sooner should I in Paris look to see
An English army sent their guard to be.'
"My poor mamma, who had her mind subdued
By whig-control, and hated every feud,
Would have her neighbour met with mind serene;
But fiercer spirit fired the tory-queen.
My parents both had given her high disgust,
Which she resenting said, 'Revenge is just;'
And till th' offending parties chose to stoop,
She judged it right to keep resentment up;
Could she in friendship with a woman live
Who could the insult of a man forgive?
Did not her husband in a crowded room
Once call her idiot, and the thing was dumb?
The man's attack was brutal to be sure,
But she no less an idiot to endure.
"This lofty dame, with unrelenting soul,

Had a fair girl to govern and control;
The dear Maria!—whom, when first I met,—
Shame on this weakness! do I feel it yet?
"The parents' anger, you will oft-times see,
Prepares the children's minds for amity;
Youth will not enter into such debate;
'Tis not in them to cherish groundless hate;
Nor can they feel men's quarrels or their cares,
Of whig or tory, partridges or hares.
"Long ere we loved, this gentle girl and I
Gave to our parents' discord many a sigh;
It was not ours—and, when the meeting came,
It pleased us much to find our thoughts the same;
But grief and trouble in our minds arose
From the fierce spirits we could not compose;
And much it vex'd us that the friends so dear
To us should foes among themselves appear.
"Such was this maid, the angel of her race,
Whom I had loved in any time and place,
But in a time and place which chance assign'd,
When it was almost treason to be kind;
When we had vast impediments in view,
Then wonder not that love in terror grew
With double speed—we look'd, and strove to find
A kindred spirit in the hostile mind;
But is it hostile? there appears no sign
In those dear looks of warfare—none have mine;
At length I whisper'd—'Would that war might cease
Between our houses, and that all was peace!'
A sweet confusion on her features rose,
'She could not bear to think of having foes,
When we might all as friends and neighbours live,
And for that blessing, O! what would she give!'—
'Then let us try and our endeavours blend,'
I said, 'to bring these quarrels to an end.'
Thus, with one purpose in our hearts, we strove,
And, if no more, increased our secret love:
Love that, with such impediments in view,
To meet the growing danger stronger grew;
And from that time each heart, resolved and sure,
Grew firm in hope, and patient to endure.
"To those who know this season of delight
I need not strive their feelings to excite;
To those who know not the delight or pain,
The best description would be lent in vain;
And to the grieving, who will no more find
The bower of bliss, to paint it were unkind.
I pass it by, to tell that long we tried

To bring our fathers over to our side;
'Twas bootless on their wives our skill to try,
For one would not, and one in vain, comply.
"First I began my father's heart to move,
By boldly saying 'We are born to love;'
My father answer'd, with an air of ease,
'Well! very well! be loving if you please!
Except a man insults us or offends,
In my opinion we should all be friends.'
"This gain'd me nothing; little would accrue
From clearing points so useless though so true;
But with some pains I brought him to confess,
That to forgive our wrongs is to redress.
"'It might be so,' he answer'd, yet with doubt
That it might not; 'but what is this about?'
I dared not speak directly, but I strove
To keep my subjects, harmony and love.
"Coolly my father look'd, and much enjoy'd
The broken eloquence his eye destroy'd;
Yet less confused, and more resolved at last,
With bolder effort to my point I past;
And, fondly speaking of my peerless maid,
I call'd her worth and beauty to my aid;
'Then make her mine!' I said, and for his favour pray'd.
"My father's look was one I seldom saw;
It gave no pleasure, nor created awe:
It was the kind of cool contemptuous smile
Of witty persons, overcharged with bile;
At first he spoke not, nor at last to me—
"'Well now, and what if such a thing could be?
What, if the boy should his addresses pay
To the tall girl, would that old tory say?
I have no hatred to the dog—but, still,
It was some pleasure when I used him ill;
This I must lose if we should brethren be,
Yet may be not, for brethren disagree;
The fool is right—there is no bar in life
Against their marriage—let her be his wife.—
Well, sir, you hear me!'—Never man complied,
And left a beggar so dissatisfied;
Though all was granted, yet was grace refused;
I felt as one indulged, and yet abused;
And yet, although provoked, I was not unamused.
"In a reply like this appear'd to meet
All that encourage hope, and that defeat;
Consent, though cool, had been for me enough,
But this consent had something of reproof;
I had prepared my answer to his rage,

With his contempt I thought not to engage.
I, like a hero, would my castle storm,
And meet the giant in his proper form;
Then, conquering him, would set my princess free:
This would a trial and a triumph be—
When lo! a sneering menial brings the keys,
And cries in scorn, 'Come, enter, if you please;
You'll find the lady sitting on her bed,
And 'tis expected that you woo and wed.'
"Yet not so easy was my conquest found;
I met with trouble ere with triumph crown'd.
Triumph, alas!—My father little thought.
A king at home, how other minds are wrought;
True, his meek neighbour was a gentle squire,
And had a soul averse from wrath and ire;
He answer'd frankly, when to him I went,
'I give you little, sir, in my consent.'
He and my mother were to us inclined,
The powerless party with the peaceful mind;
But that meek man was destined to obey
A sovereign lady's unremitted sway,
Who bore no partial, no divided rule;
All were obedient pupils in her school.
She had religious zeal, both strong and sour,
That gave an active sternness to her power;
But few could please her—she herself was one
By whom that deed was very seldom done.
With such a being, so disposed to feed
Contempt and scorn—how was I to succeed?
But love commanded, and I made my prayer
To the stern lady, with an humble air,
Said all that lovers hope, all measures tried
That love suggested, and bow'd down to pride.
"Yes! I have now the tygress in my eye—
When I had ceased and waited her reply,
A pause ensued; and then she slowly rose
With bitter smile predictive of my woes,
A look she saw was plainly understood—
"'Admire my daughter! Sir, you're very good.
The girl is decent, take her all in all—
Genteel, we hope—perhaps a thought too tall;
A daughter's portion hers—you'll think her fortune small.
Perhaps her uncles, in a cause so good,
Would do a little for their flesh and blood;
We are not ill allied—and, say we make
Her portion decent, whither would you take?
Is there some cottage on your father's ground,
Where may a dwelling for the girl be found?

Or a small farm—your mother understands
How to make useful such a pair of hands.
"'But this we drop at present, if you please;
We shall have leisure for such things as these;
They will be proper ere you fix the day
For the poor girl to honour and obey;
At present therefore we may put an end
To our discourse—Good morrow to you, friend!'
"Then, with a solemn curtesy and profound,
Her laughing eye she lifted from the ground,
And left me lost in thought, and gazing idly round.—
"Still we had hope, and, growing bold in time,
I would engage the father in our crime;
But he refused, for, though he wish'd us well,
He said, 'he must not make his house a hell;'—
And sure the meaning look that I convey'd
Did not inform him that the hell was made.
"Still hope existed that a mother's heart
Would in a daughter's feelings take a part;
Nor was it vain—for there is found access
To a hard heart, in time of its distress.
"The mother sicken'd, and the daughter sigh'd,
And we petition'd till our queen complied;
She thought of dying, and, if power must cease,
Better to make, than cause, th' expected peace;
And sure, this kindness mixing with the blood,
Its balmy influence caused the body's good;
For as a charm it work'd upon the frame
Of the reviving and relenting dame;
For, when recover'd, she no more opposed
Her daughter's wishes.—Here contention closed.
"Then bliss ensued, so exquisitely sweet,
That with it once, once only, we can meet;
For, though we love again, and though once more
We feel th' enlivening hope we felt before,
Still the pure freshness of the joy that cast
Its sweet around us is for ever past.
O! time to memory precious—ever dear,
Though ever painful—this eventful year;
What bliss is now in view! and now what woes appear!
Sweet hours of expectation!—I was gone
To the vile town to press our business on;
To urge its formal instruments—and lo!
Comes with dire looks a messenger of wo,
With tidings sad as death!—With all my speed
I reach'd her home!—but that pure soul was freed—
She was no more—for ever shut that eye,
That look'd all soul, as if it could not die;

It could not see me—O! the strange distress
Of these new feelings!—misery's excess,
What can describe it? words will not express.
When I look back upon that dreadful scene,
I feel renew'd the anguish that has been,
And reason trembles—Yes! you bid me cease,
Nor try to think; but I will think in peace.—
Unbid and unforbidden, to the room
I went, a gloomy wretch amid that gloom;
And there the lovely being on her bed
Shrouded and cold was laid—Maria dead!
There was I left—and I have now no thought
Remains with me, how fear or fancy wrought;
I know I gazed upon the marble cheek,
And pray'd the dear departed girl to speak—
Further I know not, for, till years were fled,
All was extinguish'd—all with her was dead.
I had a general terror, dread of all
That could a thinking, feeling man befall;
I was desirous from myself to run,
And something, but I knew not what, to shun.
There was a blank from this I cannot fill;
It is a puzzle and a terror still.
Yet did I feel some intervals of bliss,
Ev'n with the horrors of a fate like this;
And dreams of wonderful construction paid
For waking horror—dear angelic maid!
"When peace return'd, unfelt for many a year,
And hope, discarded flatterer, dared t' appear;
I heard of my estate, how free from debt,
And of the comforts life afforded yet;
Beside that best of comforts in a life
So sad as mine—a fond and faithful wife.
My gentle mother, now a widow, made
These strong attempts to guide me or persuade.
"'Much time is lost,' she said, 'but yet my son
May, in the race of life, have much to run;
When I am gone, thy life to thee will seem
Lonely and sad, a melancholy dream;
Get thee a wife—I will not say to love,
But one, a friend in thy distress to prove;
One who will kindly help thee to sustain
Thy spirit's burden in its hours of pain:
Say, will you marry?'—I in haste replied,
'And who would be the self-devoted bride?
There is a melancholy power that reigns
Tyrant within me—who would bear his chains,
And hear them clicking every wretched hour,

With will to aid me, but without the power?
But if such one were found with easy mind,
Who would not ask for raptures—I'm resign'd.'
""'Tis quite enough,' my gentle mother cried;
'We leave the raptures, and will find the bride.'
"There was a lady near us, quite discreet,
Whom in our visits 'twas our chance to meet:
One grave and civil, who had no desire
That men should praise her beauties or admire;
She in our walks would sometimes take my arm,
But had no foolish fluttering or alarm;
She wish'd no heart to wound, no truth to prove,
And seem'd, like me, as one estranged from love;
My mother praised her, and with so much skill,
She gave a certain bias to my will;
But calm indeed our courtship; I profess'd
A due regard—My mother did the rest:
Who soon declared that we should love, and grow
As fond a couple as the world could show;
And talk'd of boys and girls with so much glee,
That I began to wish the thing could be.
"Still, when the day that soon would come was named,
I felt a cold fit, and was half ashamed;
But we too far proceeded to revoke,
And had been much too serious for a joke;
I shook away the fear that man annoys,
And thought a little of the girls and boys.
"A week remain'd—for seven succeeding days
Nor man nor woman might control my ways;
For seven dear nights I might to rest retire
At my own time, and none the cause require;
For seven blest days I might go in and out,
And none demand, 'Sir, what are you about?'
For one whole week I might at will discourse
On any subject, with a freeman's force.
"Thus while I thought, I utter'd, as men sing
In under-voice, reciting 'With this ring;'
That, when the hour should come, I might not dread
These, or the words that follow'd, 'I thee wed.'
"Such was my state of mind, exulting now
And then depress'd—I cannot tell you how—
When a poor lady, whom her friends could send
On any message, a convenient friend,
Who had all feelings of her own o'ercome,
And could pronounce to any man his doom;
Whose heart indeed was marble, but whose face
Assumed the look adapted to the case,
Enter'd my room, commission'd to assuage

What was foreseen, my sorrow and my rage.
"It seem'd the lady whom I could prefer,
And could my much-loved freedom lose for her,
Had bold attempts, but not successful, made,
The heart of some rich cousin to invade;
Who, half resisting, half complying, kept
A cautious distance, and the business slept.
"This prudent swain his own importance knew,
And swore to part the now affianced two.
Fill'd with insidious purpose, forth he went,
Profess'd his love, and woo'd her to consent.
'Ah! were it true!' she sigh'd; he boldly swore
His love sincere, and mine was sought no more.
"All this the witch at dreadful length reveal'd,
And begg'd me calmly to my fate to yield:
Much pains she took engagements old to state,
And hoped to hear me curse my cruel fate,
Threat'ning my luckless life; and thought it strange
In me to bear the unexpected change;
In my calm feelings she beheld disguise,
And told of some strange wildness in my eyes.
"But there was nothing in the eye amiss,
And the heart calmly bore a stroke like this.
Not so my mother; though of gentle kind,
She could no mercy for the creature find.
"'Vile plot!' she said.—'But, madam, if they plot,
And you would have revenge, disturb them not.'—
"'What can we do, my son?'—'Consult our ease,
And do just nothing, madam, if you please.'—
"'What will be said?'—'We need not that discuss;
Our friends and neighbours will do that for us.'—
"'Do you so lightly, son, your loss sustain?'—
'Nay, my dear madam, but I count it gain.'—
"'The world will blame us sure, if we be still.'—
'And, if we stir, you may be sure it will.'—
"'Not to such loss your father had agreed.'—
'No, for my father's had been loss indeed.'
"With gracious smile my mother gave assent,
And let th' affair slip by with much content.
"Some old dispute, the lover meant should rise,
Some point of strife they could not compromise,
Displeased the squire—he from the field withdrew,
Not quite conceal'd, not fully placed in view;
But half advancing, half retreating, kept
At his old distance, and the business slept.
"Six years had past, and forty ere the six,
When Time began to play his usual tricks:
The locks once comely in a virgin's sight,

Locks of pure brown, display'd th' encroaching white;
The blood once fervid now to cool began,
And Time's strong pressure to subdue the man.
I rode or walk'd as I was wont before,
But now the bounding spirit was no more;
A moderate pace would now my body heat,
A walk of moderate length distress my feet.
I show'd my stranger-guest those hills sublime,
But said, 'the view is poor, we need not climb.'
At a friend's mansion I began to dread
The cold neat parlour, and the gay glazed bed;
At home I felt a more decided taste,
And must have all things in my order placed;
I ceased to hunt, my horses pleased me less,
My dinner more; I learn'd to play at chess;
I took my dog and gun, but saw the brute
Was disappointed that I did not shoot;
My morning walks I now could bear to lose,
And bless'd the shower that gave me not to choose:
In fact, I felt a languor stealing on;
The active arm, the agile hand were gone;
Small daily actions into habits grew,
And new dislike to forms and fashion new;
I loved my trees in order to dispose,
I number'd peaches, look'd how stocks arose,
Told the same story oft—in short, began to prose.
"My books were changed; I now preferred the truth
To the light reading of unsettled youth;
Novels grew tedious, but, by choice or chance,
I still had interest in the wild romance.
There is an age, we know, when tales of love
Form the sweet pabulum our hearts approve;
Then as we read we feel, and are indeed,
We judge, th' heroic men of whom we read;
But in our after life these fancies fail;
We cannot be the heroes of the tale;
The parts that Cliffords, Mordaunts, Bevilles play
We cannot—cannot be so smart and gay.
"But all the mighty deeds and matchless powers
Of errant knights we never fancied ours,
And thus the prowess of each gifted knight
Must at all times create the same delight;
Lovelace a forward youth might hope to seem,
But Lancelot never—that he could not dream;
Nothing reminds us in the magic page
Of old romance, of our declining age.
If once our fancy mighty dragons slew,
This is no more than fancy now can do;

But when the heroes of a novel come,
Conquer'd and conquering, to a drawing-room,
We no more feel the vanity that sees
Within ourselves what we admire in these;
And so we leave the modern tale, to fly
From realm to realm with Tristram or Sir Guy.
"Not quite a Quixote, I could not suppose
That queens would call me to subdue their foes;
But, by a voluntary weakness sway'd,
When fancy call'd, I willingly obey'd.
"Such became, and I believed my heart
Might yet be pierced by some peculiar dart
Of right heroic kind, and I could prove
Fond of some peerless nymph who deign'd to love,
Some high-soul'd virgin, who had spent her time
In studies grave, heroic and sublime;
Who would not like me less that I had spent
Years eight and forty, just the age of Kent—
But not with Kent's discretion, for I grew
Fond of a creature whom my fancy drew:
A kind of beings who are never found
On middle-earth, but grow on fairy-ground.
"These found I not; but I had luck to find
A mortal woman of this fairy kind;
A thin, tall, upright, serious, slender maid,
Who in my own romantic regions stray'd;
From the world's glare to this sweet vale retired,
To dwell unseen, unsullied, unadmired;
In all her virgin excellence, above
The gaze of crowds, and hopes of vulgar love.
"We spoke of noble deeds in happier times,
Of glorious virtues, of debasing crimes.
Warm was the season, and the subject too,
And therefore warm in our discourse we grew.
Love made such haste, that ere a month was flown
Since first we met, he had us for his own:
Riches are trifles in an hero's sight,
And lead to questions low and unpolite;
I nothing said of money or of land,
But bent my knee, and fondly ask'd her hand;
And the dear lady, with a grace divine,
Gave it, and frankly answer'd, 'it is thine.'
"Our reading was not to romance confined,
But still it gave its colour to the mind;
Gave to our studies something of its force,
And made profound and tender our discourse;
Our subjects all, and our religion, took
The grave and solemn spirit of our book;

And who had seen us walk, or heard us read,
Would say, 'these lovers are sublime indeed.'
"I knew not why, but when the day was named
My ardent wishes felt a little tamed;
My mother's sickness then awaked my grief,
And yet, to own the truth, was some relief;
It left uncertain that decisive time
That made my feelings nervous and sublime.
"Still all was kindness, and at morn and eve
I made a visit, talk'd, and took my leave:
Kind were the lady's looks, her eyes were bright,
And swam, I thought, in exquisite delight;
A lovely red suffused the virgin cheek,
And spoke more plainly than the tongue could speak;
Plainly all seem'd to promise love and joy,
Nor fear'd we ought that might our bliss destroy.
"Engaged by business, I one morn delay'd
My usual call on the accomplish'd maid;
But soon, that small impediment removed,
I paid the visit that decisive proved;
For the fair lady had, with grieving heart,
So I believed, retired to sigh apart:
I saw her friend, and begg'd her to entreat
My gentle nymph her sighing swain to meet.
"The gossip gone—What dæmon, in his spite
To love and man, could my frail mind excite,
And lead me curious on, against all sense of right?
There met my eye, unclosed, a closet's door—
Shame! how could I the secrets there explore?
Pride, honour, friendship, love, condemn'd the deed,
And yet, in spite of all, I could proceed!
I went, I saw—Shall I describe the hoard
Of precious worth in seal'd deposits stored
Of sparkling hues? Enough—enough is told,
'Tis not for man such mysteries to unfold.
Thus far I dare—Whene'er those orbits swam
In that blue liquid that restrain'd their flame,
As showers the sunbeams—when the crimson glow
Of the red rose o'erspread those cheeks of snow,
I saw, but not the cause—'twas not the red
Of transient blush that o'er her face was spread;
'Twas not the lighter red, that partly streaks
The Catherine pear, that brighten'd o'er her cheeks,
Nor scarlet blush of shame—but such disclose
The velvet petals of the Austrian rose,
When first unfolded: warm the glowing hue,
Nor cold as rouge, but deep'ning on the view.
Such were those cheeks—the causes unexplored

Were now detected in that secret hoard;
And ever to that rich recess would turn
My mind, and cause for such effect discern.
Such was my fortune, O! my friends, and such
The end of lofty hopes that grasp'd too much.
This was, indeed, a trying time in life,
I lost at once a mother and a wife;
Yet compensation came in time for these,
And what I lost in joy, I gain'd in ease."—
"But," said the squire, "did thus your courtship cease?
Resign'd your mistress her betroth'd in peace?"—
"Yes; and had sense her feelings to restrain,
Nor ask'd me once my conduct to explain;
But me she saw those swimming eyes explore,
And explanation she required no more.
Friend to the last, I left her with regret—
Nay, leave her not, for we are neighbours yet.
"These views extinct, I travell'd, not with taste,
But so that time ran wickedly to waste;
I penn'd some notes, and might a book have made,
But I had no connexion with the trade;
Bridges and churches, towers and halls, I saw,
Maids and madonnas, and could sketch and draw:
Yes, I had made a book, but that my pride
In the not making was more gratified.
"There was one feeling upon foreign ground,
That more distressing than the rest was found:
That, though with joy I should my country see,
There none had pleasure in expecting me.
"I now was sixty, but could walk and eat;
My food was pleasant, and my slumbers sweet;
But what could urge me at a day so late
To think of women?—my unlucky fate.
It was not sudden; I had no alarms,
But was attack'd when resting on my arms;
Like the poor soldier: when the battle raged
The man escaped, though twice or thrice engaged;
But, when it ended, in a quiet spot
He fell, the victim of a random-shot.
"With my good friend the vicar oft I spent
The evening hours in quiet, as I meant;
He was a friend in whom, although untried
By ought severe, I found I could confide;
A pleasant, sturdy disputant was he,
Who had a daughter—such the Fates decree,
To prove how weak is man—poor yielding man, like me.
"Time after time the maid went out and in,
Ere love was yet beginning to begin;

The first awakening proof, the early doubt,
Rose from observing she went in and out.
My friend, though careless, seem'd my mind to explore,
'Why do you look so often at the door?'
I then was cautious, but it did no good,
For she, at least, my meanings understood;
But to the vicar nothing she convey'd
Of what she thought—she did not feel afraid.
"I must confess, this creature in her mind
Nor face had beauty that a man would blind;
No poet of her matchless charms would write,
Yet sober praise they fairly would excite.
She was a creature form'd man's heart to make
Serenely happy, not to pierce and shake;
If she were tried for breaking human hearts,
Men would acquit her—she had not the arts.
Yet without art, at first without design,
She soon became the arbitress of mine;
Without pretensions—nay, without pretence,
But by a native strange intelligence
Women possess when they behold a man
Whom they can tease, and are assured they can;
Then 'tis their soul's delight and pride to reign
O'er the fond slave, to give him ease or pain,
And stretch and loose by turns the weighty viewless chain,
"Though much she knew, yet nothing could she prove;
I had not yet confess'd the crime of love;
But, in an hour when guardian-angels sleep,
I fail'd the secret of my soul to keep;
And then I saw the triumph in those eyes
That spoke—'Ay, now you are indeed my prize.'
I almost thought I saw compassion, too,
For all the cruel things she meant to do.
Well I can call to mind the managed air
That gave no comfort, that brought no despair,
That in a dubious balance held the mind,
To each side turning, never much inclined.
"She spoke with kindness—thought the honour high,
And knew not how to give a fit reply;
She could not, would not, dared not, must not deem
Such language proof of ought but my esteem;
It made her proud—she never could forget
My partial thoughts—she felt her much in debt:
She who had never in her life indulged
The thought of hearing what I now divulged:
I, who had seen so many and so much—
It was an honour—she would deem it such.
Our different years, indeed, would put an end

To other views, but still her father's friend
To her, she humbly hoped, would his regard extend.
Thus, saying nothing, all she meant to say,
She play'd the part the sex delights to play;
Now by some act of kindness giving scope
To the new workings of excited hope,
Then by an air of something like disdain,
But scarcely seen, repelling it again;
Then for a season, neither cold nor kind,
She kept a sort of balance in the mind,
And, as his pole a dancer on the rope,
The equal poise on both sides kept me up.
"Is it not strange that man can fairly view
Pursuit like this, and yet his point pursue;
While he the folly fairly will confess,
And even feel the danger of success?
But so it is, and nought the Circes care
How ill their victims with their poison fare,
When thus they trifle, and with quiet soul
Mix their ingredients in the maddening bowl:
Their high regard, the softness of their air,
The pitying grief that saddens at a prayer,
Their grave petitions for the peace of mind
That they determine you shall never find,
And all their vain amazement that a man
Like you should love—they wonder how you can.
"For months the idler play'd her wicked part,
Then fairly gave the secret of her heart.
'She hoped'—I now the smiling gipsy view—
'Her father's friend would be her lover's too;
Young Henry Gale'—'But why delay so long?'—
'She could not tell—she fear'd it might be wrong,
But I was good'—I knew not, I was weak,
And spoke as love directed me to speak.
"When in my arms their boy and girl I take,
I feel a fondness for the mother's sake;
But though the dears some softening thoughts excite,
I have no wishes for the father's right.
"Now all is quiet, and the mind sustains
Its proper comforts, its befitting pains;
The heart reposes; it has had its share
Of love, as much as it could fairly bear;
And what is left in life that now demands its care?
"For O! my friends, if this were all indeed;
Could we believe that nothing would succeed;
If all were but this daily dose of life,
Without a care or comfort, child or wife;
These walks for health with nothing more in view;

This doing nothing, and with labour too;
This frequent asking when 'tis time to dine;
This daily dosing o'er the news and wine;
This age's riddle, when each day appears
So very long, so very short the years;
If this were all—but let me not suppose—
What then were life! whose virtues, trials, woes,
Would sleep th' eternal sleep, and there the scene would close.
"This cannot be—but why has Time a pace
That seems unequal in our mortal race?
Quick is that pace in early life, but slow,
Tedious and heavy, as we older grow;
But yet, though slow, the movements are alike,
And with no force upon the memory strike,
And therefore tedious as we find them all,
They leave us nothing we in view recal;
But days that we so dull and heavy knew
Are now as moments passing in review,
And hence arises ancient men's report,
That days are tedious, and yet years are short."

TALES OF THE HALL

BOOK XI

THE MAID'S STORY
—

TALES OF THE HALL

BOOK XI

THE MAID'S STORY

Three days remain'd their friend, and then again
The Brothers left themselves to entertain;
When spake the younger—"It would please me well

To hear thy spinster-friend her story tell;
And our attention would be nobly paid
Thus to compare the Bachelor and Maid."
"Frank as she is," replied the squire, "nor one
Is more disposed to show what she has done
With time, or time with her: yet all her care
And every trial she might not declare
To one a stranger; but to me, her friend,
She has the story of those trials penn'd;
These shalt thou hear, for well the maid I know,
And will her efforts and her conquests show.
Jacques is abroad, and we alone shall dine,
And then to give this lady's tale be mine;
Thou wilt attend to this good spinster's life,
And grieve and wonder she is not a wife;
But if we judge by either words or looks,
Her mode of life, her morals, or her books,
Her pure devotion, unaffected sense,
Her placid air, her mild benevolence,
Her gay good humour, and her manners free,
She is as happy as a maid can be;
If as a wife, I know not, and decline
Question like this, till I can judge of thine."

Then from a secret hoard drew forth the squire
His tale, and said, "Attention I require—
My verse you may condemn, my theme you must admire."

I to your kindness speak, let that prevail,
And of my frailty judge as beings frail.—
My father, dying, to my mother left
An infant charge, of all things else bereft;
Poor, but experienced in the world, she knew
What others did, and judged what she could do;
Beauty she justly weigh'd, was never blind
To her own interest, and she read mankind:
She view'd my person with approving glance,
And judged the way my fortune to advance;
Taught me betimes that person to improve,
And make a lawful merchandize of love;
Bade me my temper in subjection keep,
And not permit my vigilance to sleep;
I was not one, a miss, who might presume
Now to be crazed by mirth, now sunk in gloom;
Nor to be fretful, vapourish, or give way
To spleen and anger, as the wealthy may;
But I must please, and all I felt of pride,
Contempt, and hatred, I must cast aside.

"Have not one friend," my mother cried, "not one;
That bane of our romantic triflers shun;
Suppose her true, can she afford you aid?
Suppose her false, your purpose is betray'd;
And then in dubious points, and matters nice,
How can you profit by a child's advice?
While you are writing on from post to post,
Your hour is over, and a man is lost;
Girls of their hearts are scribbling, their desires,
And what the folly of the heart requires,
Dupes to their dreams—but I the truth impart,
You cannot, child, afford to have a heart.
Think nothing of it; to yourself be true,
And keep life's first great business in your view—
Take it, dear Martha, for a useful rule,
She who is poor is ugly or a fool;
Or, worse than either, has a bosom fill'd
With soft emotions, and with raptures thrill'd.
"Read not too much, nor write in verse or prose,
For then you make the dull and foolish foes;
Yet those who do deride not nor condemn,
It is not safe to raise up foes in them;
For though they harm you not, as blockheads do,
There is some malice in the scribbling crew."
Such her advice; full hard with her had dealt
The world, and she the usage keenly felt.
"Keep your good name," she said, "and that to keep
You must not suffer vigilance to sleep.
Some have, perhaps, the name of chaste retain'd,
When nought of chastity itself remain'd;
But there is danger—few have means to blind
The keen-eyed world, and none to make it kind.
"And one thing more—to free yourself from foes
Never a secret to your friend disclose;
Secrets with girls, like loaded guns with boys,
Are never valued till they make a noise;
To show how trusted, they their power display;
To show how worthy, they the trust betray;
Like pence in children's pockets secrets lie
In female bosoms—they must burn or fly.
"Let not your heart be soften'd; if it be,
Let not the man his softening influence see;
For the most fond will sometimes tyrants prove,
And wound the bosom where they trace the love.
But to your fortune look, on that depend
For your life's comfort; comforts that attend
On wealth alone—wealth gone, they have their end."
Such were my mother's cares to mend my lot,

And such her pupil they succeeded not.
It was conceived the person I had then
Might lead to serious thoughts some wealthy men,
Who, having none their purpose to oppose,
Would soon be won their wishes to disclose.
My mother thought I was the very child
By whom the old and amorous are beguiled:
So mildly gay, so ignorantly fair,
And pure, no doubt, as sleeping infants are;
Then had lessons how to look and move,
And, I repeat, make merchandize of love.
Thrice it was tried if one so young could bring
Old wary men to buy the binding ring;
And on the taper finger, to whose tip
The fond old swain would press his withering lip,
Place the strong charm:—and one would win my heart
By re-assuming youth—a trying part;
Girls, he supposed, all knew the young were bold,
And he would show that spirit in the old;
In boys they loved to hear the rattling tongue,
And he would talk as idly as the young;
He knew the vices our Lotharios boast,
And he would show of every vice the ghost,
The ev'l's self, without disguise or dress,
Vice in its own pure native ugliness:
Not, as the drunkenness of slaves, to prove
Vice hateful, but that seeing, I might love.
He drove me out, and I was pleased to see
Care of himself: it served as care for me;
For he would tell me, that he should not spare
Man, horse, or carriage, if I were not there:
Provoked at last, my malice I obey'd,
And smiling said, "Sir, I am not afraid."
This check'd his spirit; but he said, "Could you
Have charge so rich, you would be careful too."
And he, indeed, so very slowly drove,
That we dismiss'd the over-cautious love.
My next admirer was of equal age,
And wish'd the child's affection to engage,
And keep the fluttering bird a victim in his cage.
He had no portion of his rival's glee,
But gravely praised the gravity in me;
Religious, moral, both in word and deed,
But warmly disputatious in his creed;
Wild in his younger time, as we were told,
And therefore like a penitent when old.
Strange he should wish a lively girl to look
Upon the methods his repentance took!

Then he would say, he was no more a rake
To squander money for his passions' sake;
Yet, upon proper terms, as man discreet,
He with my mother was disposed to treat,
To whom he told, "the price of beauty fell
In every market, and but few could sell;
That trade in India, once alive and brisk,
Was over done, and scarcely worth the risk."
Then stoop'd to speak of board, and what for life
A wife would cost—if he should take a wife.
Hardly he bargain'd, and so much desired,
That we demurr'd; and he, displeased, retired.
And now I hoped to rest, nor act again
The paltry part for which I felt disdain,
When a third lover came within our view,
And somewhat differing from the former two.
He had been much abroad, and he had seen
The world's weak side, and read the hearts of men;
But all, it seem'd, this study could produce,
Was food for spleen, derision, and abuse;
He levell'd all, as one who had intent
To clear the vile and spot the innocent;
He praised my sense, and said I ought to be
From girl's restraint and nursery maxims free;
He praised my mother; but he judged her wrong
To keep us from th' admiring world so long;
He praised himself; and then his vices named,
And call'd them follies, and was not ashamed.
He more than hinted that the lessons taught
By priests were all with superstition fraught;
And I must think them for the crowd design'd,
Not to alarm the free and liberal mind.
Wisdom with him was virtue. They were wrong
And weak, he said, who went not with the throng;
Man must his passions order and restrain
In all that gives his fellow-subjects pain;
But yet of guilt he would in pity speak,
And as he judged, the wicked were the weak.
Such was the lover of a simple maid,
Who seem'd to call his logic to his aid,
And to mean something; I will not pretend
To judge the purpose of my reasoning friend,
Who was dismiss'd, in quiet to complain
That so much labour was bestow'd in vain.
And now my mother seem'd disposed to try
A life of reason and tranquillity.
Ere this, her health and spirits were the best,
Hers the day's trifling, and the nightly rest;

But something new was in her mind instill'd;
Unquiet thoughts the matron bosom fill'd;
For five and forty peaceful years she bore
Her placid looks, and dress becoming wore:
She could a compliment with pleasure take,
But no absurd impression could it make.
Now were her nerves disorder'd; she was weak,
And must the help of a physician seek:
A Scotch physician, who had just began
To settle near us, quite a graceful man,
And very clever, with a soft address,
That would his meaning tenderly express.
Sick as my mother seem'd, when he inquired
If she was ill, he found her well attired;
She purchased wares so showy and so fine,
The venders all believed th' indulgence mine;—
But I, who thrice was woo'd, had lovers three,
Must now again a very infant be;
While the good lady, twenty years a wife,
Was to decide the colour of his life:
And she decided. She was wont t' appear
To these unequal marriages severe;
Her thoughts of such with energy she told,
And was repulsive, dignified, and cold;
But now, like monarchs weary of a throne,
She would no longer reign—at least alone.
She gave her pulse, and, with a manner sweet,
Wish'd him to feel how kindly they could beat;
And 'tis a thing quite wonderful to tell
How soon he understood them, and how well.
Now, when she married, I from home was sent,
With grandmamma to keep perpetual Lent;
For she would take me on conditions cheap,
For what we scarcely could a parrot keep:
A trifle added to the daily fare
Would feed a maiden who must learn to spare.
With grandmamma I lived in perfect ease;
Consent to starve, and I was sure to please.
Full well I knew the painful shifts we made
Expenses all to lessen or evade,
And tradesmen's flinty hearts to soften and persuade.
Poor grandmamma among the gentry dwelt
Of a small town, and all the honour felt;
Shrinking from all approaches to disgrace
That might be mark'd in so genteel a place;
Where every daily deed, as soon as done,
Ran through the town as fast as it could run—
At dinners what appear'd—at cards who lost or won

Our good appearance through the town was known,
Hunger and thirst were matters of our own;
And you would judge that she in scandal dealt
Who told on what we fed, or how we felt.
We had a little maid, some four feet high,
Who was employ'd our household stores to buy;
For she would weary every man in trade,
And tease t' assent whom she could not persuade.
Methinks I see her, with her pigmy light,
Precede her mistress in a moonless night;
From the small lantern throwing through the street
The dimm'd effulgence at her lady's feet;
What time she went to prove her well-known skill
With rival friends at their beloved quadrille.
"And how's your pain?" inquired the gentle maid,
For that was asking if with luck she play'd;
And this she answer'd as the cards decreed,
"O Biddy! ask not—very bad indeed;"
Or, in more cheerful tone, from spirit light,
"Why, thank you, Biddy, pretty well to-night."
The good old lady often thought me vain,
And of my dress would tenderly complain;
But liked my taste in food of every kind,
As from all grossness, like her own, refined.
Yet when she hinted that on herbs and bread
Girls of my age and spirit should be fed,
Whate'er my age had borne, my flesh and blood,
Spirit and strength, the interdict withstood;
But, though I might the frugal soul offend
Of the good matron, now my only friend,
And though her purse suggested rules so strict,
Her love could not the punishment inflict;
She sometimes watch'd the morsel with a frown,
And sigh'd to see, but let it still go down.
Our butcher's bill, to me a monstrous sum,
Was such that, summon'd, he forbore to come:
Proud man was he, and when the bill was paid,
He put the money in his bag and play'd,
Jerking it up, and catching it again,
And poising in his hand in pure disdain;
While the good lady, awed by man so proud,
And yet disposed to have her claims allow'd,
Balanced between humility and pride,
Stood a fall'n empress at the butcher's side,
Praising his meat as delicate and nice—
"Yes, madam, yes! if people pay the price."
So lived the lady, and so murmur'd I,
In all the grief of pride and poverty.

Twice in the year there came a note to tell
How well mamma, who hoped the child was well;
It was not then a pleasure to be styled,
By a mamma of such experience, 'Child!'
But I suppressed the feelings of my pride,
Or other feelings set them all aside.
There was a youth from college, just the one
I judged mamma would value as a son;
He was to me good, handsome, learn'd, genteel,
I cannot now what then I thought reveal;
But, in a word, he was the very youth
Who told me what I judged the very truth,
That love like his and charms like mine agreed,
For all description they must both exceed.
Yet scarcely can I throw a smile on things
So painful, but that Time his comfort brings,
Or rather throws oblivion on the mind,
For we are more forgetful than resign'd.
We both were young, had heard of love and read,
And could see nothing in the thing to dread,
But like a simple pair our time employ'd
In pleasant views to be in time enjoy'd.
When Frederick came, the kind old lady smiled
To see the youth so taken with her child;
A nice young man, who came with unsoil'd feet
In her best room, and neither drank nor eat.
Alas! he planted in a vacant breast
The hopes and fears that robb'd it of its rest.
All now appear'd so right, so fair, so just,
We surely might the lovely prospect trust;
Alas! poor Frederick and his charmer found
That they were standing on fallacious ground:
All that the father of the youth could do
Was done—and now he must himself pursue
Success in life; and, honest truth to state,
He was not fitted for a candidate.
I, too, had nothing in this world below,
Save what a Scotch physician could bestow,
Who for a pittance took my mother's hand;
And, if disposed, what had they to command?
But these were after fears, nor came t' annoy
The tender children in their dreams of joy;
Who talk'd of glebe and garden, tithe and rent,
And how a fancied income should be spent;
What friends, what social parties we should see,
And live with what genteel economy;
In fact, we gave our hearts as children give,
And thought of living as our neighbours live.

Now, when assured ourselves that all was well,
'Twas right our friends of these designs to tell;
For this we parted.—Grandmamma, amazed,
Upon her child with fond compassion gazed;
Then pious tears appear'd, but not a word
In aid of weeping till she cried, "Good Lord!"
She then, with hurried motion, sought the stairs,
And, calling Biddy, bade her come to prayers.
Yet the good lady early in her life
Was call'd to vow the duties of a wife;
She sought the altar by her friends' advice,
No free-will offering, but a sacrifice;
But here a forward girl and eager boy
Dared talk of life, and turn their heads with joy!
To my mamma I wrote in just the way
I felt, and said what dreaming lasses say:
How handsome Frederick was, by all confess'd,
How well he look'd, how very well he dress'd;
With learning much, that would for both provide,
His mother's darling, and his father's pride;
'And then he loves me more than mind can guess,
Than heart conceive, or eloquence express.'
No letter came a doubtful mind to ease,
And, what was worse, no Frederick came to please;
To college gone—so thought our little maid—
But not to see me! I was much afraid;
I walk'd the garden round, and deeply sigh'd,
When grandmamma grew faint! and dropt, and died:
A fate so awful and so sudden drove
All else away, and half extinguish'd love.
Strange people came; they search'd the house around,
And, vulgar wretches! sold whate'er they found:
The secret hoards that in the drawers were kept,
The silver toys that with the tokens slept,
The precious beads, the corals with their bells,
That laid secure, lock'd up in secret cells,
The costly silk, the tabby, the brocade,
The very garment for the wedding made,
Were brought to sale, with many a jest thereon!
"Going—a bridal dress—for—Going!—Gone."
That ring, dear pledge of early love and true,
That to the wedded finger almost grew,
Was sold for six and ten-pence to a Jew!
Great was the fancied worth; but ah! how small
The sum thus made, and yet how valued all!
But all that to the shameful service went
Just paid the bills, the burial, and the rent;
And I and Biddy, poor deserted maids!

Were turn'd adrift to seek for other aids.
Now left by all the world, as I believed,
I wonder'd much that I so little grieved;
Yet I was frighten'd at the painful view
Of shiftless want, and saw not what to do.
In times like this the poor have little dread,
They can but work, and they shall then be fed;
And Biddy cheer'd me with such thoughts as this,
"You'll find the poor have their enjoyments, Miss!"
Indeed I saw, for Biddy took me home
To a forsaken hovel's cold and gloom;
And while my tears in plenteous flow were shed,
With her own hands she placed her proper bed,
Reserved for need. A fire was quickly made,
And food, the purchase for the day, display'd;
She let in air to make the damps retire,
Then placed her sad companion at her fire;
She then began her wonted peace to feel,
She [brought] her wool, and sought her favourite wheel;
That as she turn'd, she sang with sober glee,
"Begone, dull Care! I'll have no more with thee";
Then turn'd to me, and bade me weep no more,
But try and taste the pleasures of the poor.
When dinner came, on table brown and bare
Were placed the humblest forms of earthen ware,
With one blue dish, on which our food was placed,
For appetite provided, not for taste.
I look'd disgusted, having lately seen
All so minutely delicate and clean;
Yet, as I sate, I found to my surprise
A vulgar kind of inclination rise,
And near my humble friend, and nearer, drew,
Tried the strange food, and was partaker too.
I walk'd at eve, but not where I was seen,
And thought, with sorrow, what can Frederick mean?
I must not write, I said, for I am poor;
And then I wept till I could weep no more.
Kind-hearted Biddy tried my griefs to heal,
This is a nothing to what others feel;
Life has a thousand sorrows worse than this,
A lover ost is not a fortune, Miss!
One goes, another comes, and which is best
There is no telling—set your heart at rest."
At night we pray'd—I dare not say a word
Of our devotion, it was so absurd;
And very pious upon Biddy's part,
But mine were all effusions of the heart;
While she her angels call'd their peace to shed,

And bless the corners of our little bed.
All was a dream! I said, is this indeed
To be my life? and thus to lodge and feed,
To pay for what I have, and work for what I need?
Must I be poor? and Frederick, if we meet,
Would not so much as know me in the street?
Or, as he walk'd with ladies, he would try
To be engaged as we were passing by—
And then I wept to think that I should grow
Like them whom he would be ashamed to know.
On the third day, while striving with my fate,
And hearing Biddy all its comforts state,
Talking of all her neighbours, all her schemes,
Her stories, merry jests, and warning dreams,
With tales of mirth and murder—O! the nights
Past, said the maiden, in such dear delights,
And I was thinking, can the time arrive
When I shall thus be humbled, and survive?—
Then I beheld a horse and handsome gig,
With the good air, tall form, and comely wig
Of Doctor Mackey—I in fear began
To say, Good heaven, preserve me from the man!
But fears ill reason—heaven to such a mind
Had lent a heart compassionate and kind.
From him I learnt that one had call'd to know
What with my hand my parents could bestow;
And when he learn'd the truth, in high disdain
He told my fate, and home return'd again.
"Nay, be not grieved, my lovely girl; but few
Wed the first love, however kind and true;
Something there comes to break the strongest vow,
Or mine had been my gentle Mattie now.
When the good lady died—but let me leave
All gloomy subjects—'tis not good to grieve."
Thus the kind Scotchman soothed me; he sustain'd
A father's part, and my submission gain'd,
Then my affection; and he often told
My sterner parent that her heart was cold.
He grew in honour—he obtain'd a name—
And now a favourite with the place became;
To me most gentle, he would condescend
To read and reason, be the guide and friend;
He taught me knowledge of the wholesome kind,
And fill'd with many a useful truth my mind.
Life's common burden daily lighter grew;
And even Frederick lessen'd in my view.
Cold and repulsive as he once appear'd,
He was by every generous act endear'd;

And, above all, that he with ardour fill'd
My soul for truth—a love by him instill'd;
Till my mamma grew jealous of a maid
To whom an husband such attention paid:
Not grossly jealous, but it gave her pain,
And she observed, "He made her daughter vain;
And what his help to one who must not look
To gain her bread by poring on a book?"
This was distress; but this, and all beside,
Was lost in grief—my kinder parent died;
When praised and loved, when joy and health he gave,
He sank lamented to an early grave;
Then love and we the parent and the child,
Lost in one grief, allied and reconciled.
Yet soon a will, that left me half his worth,
To the same spirit gave a second birth;
But 'twas a mother's spleen; and she indeed
Was sick, and sad, and had of comfort need.
I watch'd the way her anxious spirit took,
And often found her musing o'er a book;
She changed her dress, her church, her priest, her prayer,
Join'd a new sect, and sought her comforts there.
Some strange, coarse people came, and were so free
In their addresses, they offended me;
But my mamma threw all her pride away—
More humble she as more assuming they.
"And what," they said, as having power, "are now
The inward conflicts? do you strive? and how?"
Themselves confessing thoughts so new and wild,
I thought them like the visions of a child.
"Could we," they ask, "our best good deeds condemn?
And did we long to touch the garment's hem?
And was it so with us? for so it was with them."
A younger few assumed a softer part,
And tried to shake the fortress of my heart;
To this my pliant mother lent her aid,
And wish'd the winning of her erring maid.
I was constrain'd her female friends to hear;
But suffer'd not a bearded convert near;
Though more than one attempted, with their whine.
And "Sister! sister! how that heart of thine?"
But this was freedom I for ever check'd:
Mine was a heart no brother could affect.
But, "would I hear the preacher, and receive
The dropping dew of his discourse at eve?
The soft. sweet words?" I gave two precious hours
To hear of gifts and graces, helps and powers;
When a pale youth, who should dismiss the flock,

Gave to my bosom an electric shock.
While in that act, he look'd upon my face
As one in that all-equalizing place;
Nor, though he sought me, would he lay aside
Their cold, dead freedom, or their dull, sad pride.
Of his conversion he with triumph spoke,
Before he orders from a bishop took;
Then how his father's anger he had braved,
And, safe himself, his erring neighbours saved.
Me he rejoiced a sister to behold
Among the members of his favourite fold;
He had not sought me; the availing call
Demanded all his love, and had it all;
But, now thus met, it must be heaven's design.—
Indeed! I thought; it never shall be mine!—
Yes, we must wed. He was not rich: and I
Had of the earthly good a mean supply;
But it sufficed. Of his conversion then
He told, and labours in converting men;
For he was chosen all their bands among—
Another Daniel! honour'd, though so young.
He call'd me sister; show'd me that he knew
What I possess'd; and told what it would do;
My looks, I judge, express'd my full disdain;
But it was given to the man in vain:
They preach till they are proud, and pride disturbs the brain.
Is this the youth once timid, mild, polite?
How odious now, and sick'ning to the sight!
Proud that he sees, and yet so truly blind,
With all this blight and mildew on the mind!
Amazed, the solemn creature heard me vow
That I was not disposed to take him now.
"Then, art thou changed, fair maiden? changed thy heart?"
I answered, "No; but I perceive thou art."
Still was my mother sad, her nerves relax'd,
And our small income for advice was tax'd;
When I, who long'd for change and freedom, cried,
'Let sea and Sidmouth's balmy air be tried.'
And so they were, and every neighbouring scene,
That make the bosom, like the clime, serene;
Yet were her teachers loth to yield assent;
And not without the warning voice we went;
And there was secret counsel all unknown
To me—but I had counsel of my own.
And now there pass'd a portion of my time
In ease delicious, and in joy sublime—
With friends endear'd by kindness—with delight
In all that could the feeling mind excite,

Or please, excited; walks in every place
Where we could pleasure find and beauty trace,
Or views at night, where on the rocky steep
Shines the full moon, or glitters on the deep.
Yes, they were happy days; but they are fled!
All now are parted—part are with the dead!
Still it is pleasure, though 'tis mix'd with pain,
To think of joys that cannot live again—
Here cannot live; but they excite desire
Of purer kind, and heavenly thoughts inspire!
And now my mother, weaken'd in her mind,
Her will, subdued before, to me resign'd.
Wean'd from her late directors, by degrees
She sank resign'd, and only sought for ease.
In a small town upon the coast we fix'd,
Nor in amusement with associates mix'd.
My years—but other mode will I pursue,
And count my time by what I sought to do.
And was that mind at ease? could I avow
That no once leading thoughts engaged me now?
Was I convinced th' enthusiastic man
Had ruin'd what the loving boy began?
I answer doubting—I could still detect
Feelings too soft—yet him I could reject:
Feelings that came when I had least employ—
When common pleasures I could least enjoy—
When I was pacing lonely in the rays
Of a full moon, in lonely walks and ways—
When I was sighing o'er a tale's distress,
And paid attention to my Bible less.
These found, I sought my remedies for these;
I suffer'd common things my mind to please,
And common pleasures; seldom walk'd alone,
Nor when the moon upon the waters shone;
But then my candles lit, my window closed,
My needle took, and with my neighbours prosed;
And in one year—nay, ere the end of one,
My labour ended, and my love was done.
My heart at rest, I boldly look'd within,
And dared to ask it of its secret sin;
Alas! with pride it answer'd, "Look around,
And tell me where a better heart is found."
And then I traced my virtues; O! how few,
In fact, they were, and yet how vain I grew;
Thought of my kindness, condescension, ease,
My will, my wishes, nay, my power to please;
I judged me prudent, rational, discreet,
And void of folly, falsehood and deceit;

I read, not lightly, as I some had known,
But made an author's meaning all my own;
In short, what lady could a poet choose
As a superior subject for his muse?
So said my heart; and Conscience straight replied—
"I say the matter is not fairly tried:
I am offended, hurt, dissatisfied.
First of the Christian graces, let me see
What thy pretensions to humility?
Art thou prepared for trial? Wilt thou say
'I am this being,' and for judgment pray?
And, with the gallant Frenchman, wilt thou cry,
When to thy judge presented, 'thus am I—
Thus was I formed—these talents I possess'd—
So I employed them—and thou know'st the rest?'"
Thus Conscience; and she then a picture drew,
And bade me think and tremble at the view.
One I beheld—a wife, a mother—go
To gloomy scenes of wickedness and wo;
She sought her way through all things vile and base,
And made a prison a religious place;
Fighting her way—the way that angels fight
With powers of darkness—to let in the light.
Tell me, my heart, hast thou such victory won
As this, a sinner of thy sex, has done,
And calls herself a sinner? What art thou?
And where thy praise and exaltation now?
Yet is she tender, delicate, and nice,
And shrinks from all depravity and vice;
Shrinks from the ruffian gaze, the savage gloom,
That reign where guilt and misery find an home—
Guilt chain'd, and misery purchased; and with them
All we abhor, abominate, condemn—
The look of scorn, the scowl, th' insulting leer
Of shame, all fix'd on her who ventures here.
Yet all she braved! she kept her stedfast eye
On the dear cause, and brush'd the baseness by.
So would a mother press her darling child
Close to her breast, with tainted rags defiled.
But thou hast talents truly! say, the ten:
Come, let us look at their improvement then.
What hast thou done to aid thy suffering kind,
To help the sick, the deaf, the lame, the blind?
Hast thou not spent thy intellectual force
On books abstruse, in critical discourse?
Wasting in useless energy thy days,
And idly listening to their common praise,
Who can a kind of transient fame dispense,

And say—"a woman of exceeding sense."
Thus tried, and failing, the suggestions fled,
And a corrected spirit reign'd instead.
My mother yet was living; but the flame
Of life now flash'd, and fainter then became;
I made it pleasant, and was pleased to see
A parent looking as a child to me.
And now our humble place grew wond'rous gay;
Came gallant persons in their red array:
All strangers welcome there, extremely welcome they.
When in the church I saw inquiring eyes
Fix'd on my face with pleasure and surprise;
And soon a knocking at my door was heard;
And soon the lover of my youth appear'd—
Frederick, in all his glory, glad to meet,
And say, "his happiness was now complete."
He told his flight from superstitious zeal;
But first what torments he was doom'd to feel:
The tender tears he saw from women fall—
The strong persuasions of the brethren all—
The threats of crazed enthusiasts, bound to keep
The struggling mind, and awe the straying sheep—
From these, their love, their curses, and their creed
Was I by reason and exertion freed.
Then, like a man who often had been told
And was convinced success attends the bold,
His former purpose he renew'd, and swore
He never loved me half so well before:
Before he felt a something to divide
The heart, that now had not a love beside.
In earlier times had I myself amused,
And first my swain perplex'd, and then refused—
Cure for conceit; but now in purpose grave,
Strong and decisive the reply I gave.
Still he would come, and talk as idlers do,
Both of his old associates and his new;
Those who their dreams and reveries receive
For facts, and those who would not facts believe.
He now conceived that truth was hidden, placed
He knew not where, she never could be traced;
But that in every place, the world around,
Might some resemblance of the nymph be found.
Yet wise men knew these shadows to be vain,
Such as our true philosophers disdain—
"They laugh to see what vulgar minds pursue—
Truth, as a mistress, never in their view—
But there the shadow flies, and that, they cry, is true.'
Thus, at the college and the meeting train'd,

My lover seem'd his acmè to have gain'd;
With some compassion I essay'd a cure:
"If truth be hidden, why art thou so sure?"
This he mistook for tenderness, and cried,
"If sure of thee, I care not what beside!"
Compelled to silence, I, in pure disdain,
Withdrew from one so insolent and vain;
He then retired; and, I was kindly told,
In pure compassion grew estranged and cold.
My mother died; but, in my grief, drew near
A bosom friend, who dried the useless tear;
We lived together: we combined our shares
Of the world's good, and learn'd to brave its cares.
We were the ladies of the place, and found
Protection and respect the country round;
We gave, and largely, for we wish'd to live
In good repute—for this 'tis good to give;
Our annual present to the priest convey'd
Was kindly taken—we in comfort pray'd.
There none molested in the crimson pew
The worthy ladies, whom the vicar knew;
And we began to think that life might be—
Not happy all, but innocently free.
My friend in early life was bound to one
Of gentle kindred, but a younger son.
He fortune's smile with perseverance woo'd,
And wealth beneath the burning sun pursued.
There, urged by love and youthful hope, he went,
Loth; but 'twas all his fortune could present.
From hence he wrote; and, with a lover's fears,
And gloomy fondness, talk'd of future years;
To her devoted, his Priscilla found
His faithful heart still suffering with its wound,
That would not heal. A second time she heard;
And then no more; nor lover since appear'd.
Year after year the country's fleet arrived,
Confirm'd her fear, and yet her love survived;
It still was living; yet her hope was dead,
And youthful dreams, nay, youth itself, was fled;
And he was lost: so urged her friends, so she
At length believed, and thus retired with me.
She would a dedicated vestal prove,
And give her virgin vows to heaven and love;
She dwelt with fond regret on pleasures past,
With ardent hope on those that ever last;
Pious and tender, every day she view'd
With solemn joy our perfect solitude;
Her reading, that which most delighted her,

That soothed the passions, yet would gently stir;
The tender, softening, melancholy strain,
That caused not pleasure, but that vanquished pain,
In tears she read, and wept, and long'd to read again.
But other worlds were her supreme delight,
And there, it seem'd, she long'd to take her flight;
Yet patient, pensive, arm'd by thoughts sublime,
She watch'd the tardy steps of lingering time.
My friend, with face that most would handsome call,
Possess'd the charm that wins the heart of all;
And, thrice entreated by a lover's prayer,
She thrice refused him with determined air.
"No! had the world one monarch, and was he
All that the heart could wish its lord to be—
Lovely and loving, generous, brave, and true—
Vain were his hopes to waken hers anew!"
For she was wedded to ideal views,
And fancy's prospects, that she would not lose,
Would not forego to be a mortal's wife,
And wed the poor realities of life.
There was a day, ere yet the autumn closed,
When, ere her wintry wars, the earth reposed;
When from the yellow weed the feathery crown,
Light as the curling smoke, fell slowly down;
When the wing'd insect settled in our sight,
And waited wind to recommence her flight;
When the wide river was a silver sheet,
And on the ocean slept th' unanchor'd fleet;
When from our garden, as we look'd above,
There was no cloud, and nothing seem'd to move;
Then was my friend in ecstasies—she cried,
"There is, I feel there is, a world beside!
Martha, dear Martha! we shall hear not then
Of hearts distress'd by good or evil men,
But all will constant, tender, faithful be—
So had I been, and so had one with me;
But in this world the fondest and the best
Are the most tried, most troubled, and distress'd:
This is the place for trial, here we prove,
And there enjoy, the faithfulness of love.
"Nay, were he here in all the pride of youth,
With honour, valour, tenderness, and truth,
Entirely mine, yet what could I secure,
Or who one day of comfort could insure?
"No! all is closed on earth, and there is now
Nothing to break th' indissoluble vow;
But in that world will be th' abiding bliss,
That pays for every tear and sigh in this."

Such her discourse, and more refined it grew,
Till she had all her glorious dream in view;
And she would further in that dream proceed
Than I dare go, who doubtfully agreed.
Smiling I ask'd, again to draw the soul
From flight so high, and fancy to control,
"If this be truth, the lover's happier way
Is distant still to keep the purposed day;
The real bliss would mar the fancied joy,
And marriage all the dream of love destroy."
She softly smiled, and, as we gravely talk'd,
We saw a man who up the gravel walk'd—
Not quite erect, nor quite by age depress'd;
A travell'd man, and as a merchant dress'd.
Large chain of gold upon his watch he wore,
Small golden buckles on his feet he bore;
A head of gold his costly cane display'd,
And all about him love of gold betray'd.
This comely man moved onward, and a pair
Of comely maidens met with serious air;
Till one exclaim'd, and wildly look'd around,
"O heav'n, 'tis Paul!" and dropt upon the ground;
But she recover'd soon, and you must guess
What then ensued, and how much happiness.
They parted lovers, both distress'd to part;
They met as neighbours, heal'd, and whole of heart.
She in his absence look'd to heaven for bliss;
He was contented with a world like this:
And she prepared in some new state to meet
The man now seeking for some snug retreat.
He kindly told her he was firm and true,
Nor doubted her, and bade her then adieu!
"What shall I do?" the sighing maid began,
"How lost the lover! O, how gross the man!"
For the plain dealer had his wish declared,
Nor she, devoted victim! could be spared.
He spoke as one decided; she as one
Who fear'd the love, and would the lover shun.
"O Martha, sister of my soul! how dies
Each lovely view! for can I truth disguise,
That this is he? No! nothing shall persuade:
This is a man the naughty world has made,
An eating, drinking, buying, bargaining man—
And can I love him? No! I never can.
What once he was, what fancy gave beside,
Full well I know, my love was then my pride;
What time has done, what trade and travel wrought,
You see! and yet your sorrowing friend is sought;

But can I take him?"—"Take him not," I cried,
"If so averse—but why so soon decide?"
Meantime a daily guest the man appear'd,
Set all his sail, and for his purpose steer'd;
Loud and familiar, loving, fierce and free,
He overpower'd her soft timidity:
Who, weak and vain, and grateful to behold
The man was hers, and hers would be the gold—
Thus sundry motives, more than I can name,
Leagued on his part, and she a wife became.
A home was offer'd, but I knew too well
What comfort was with married friends to dwell;
I was resign'd, and had I felt distress,
Again a lover offer'd some redress.
Behold, a hero of the buskin hears
My loss, and with consoling love appears.
Frederick was now a hero on the stage,
In all its glories, rhapsody, and rage;
Again himself he offer'd, offer'd all
That his an hero of the kind can call:
He for my sake would hope of fame resign,
And leave the applause of all the world for mine.
Hard fate was Frederick's never to succeed,
Yet ever try—but so it was decreed.
His mind was weakened; he would laugh and weep,
And swore profusely I had murder'd sleep,
Had quite unmann'd him, cleft his heart in twain,
And he should never be himself again.
He was himself: weak, nervous, kind, and poor,
Ill dress'd and idle, he besieged my door;
Borrow'd,—or, worse; made verses on my charms,
And did his best to fill me with alarms.
I had some pity, and I sought the price
Of my repose—my hero was not nice:
There was a loan, and promise I should be
From all the efforts of his fondness free,
From hunger's future claims, or those of vanity.
"Yet," said he, bowing, "do to study take!
O! what a Desdemona wouldst thou make!"
Thus was my lover lost; yet even now
He claims one thought, and this we will allow.
His father lived to an extreme old age,
But never kind!—his son had left the stage,
And gain'd some office, but an humble place,
And that he lost! Want sharpen'd his disgrace,
Urged him to seek his father—but too late:
His jealous brothers watch'd and barr'd the gate.
The old man died; but there is one who pays

A moderate pension for his latter days;
Who, though assured inquiries will offend,
Is ever asking for this unknown friend:
Some partial lady, whom he hopes to find
As to his wants so to his wishes kind.
"Be still," a cool adviser sometimes writes—
"Nay, but," says he, "the gentle maid invites—
Do, let me know the young! the soft! the fair!"
"Old man," 'tis answer'd, "take thyself to prayer!
Be clean, be sober, to thy priest apply,
And—dead to all around thee—learn to die!"
Now had I rest from life's strong hopes and fears,
And no disturbance mark'd the flying years;
So on in quiet might those years have past,
But for a light adventure, and a last.
A handsome boy, from school-day bondage free,
Came with mamma to gaze upon the sea;
With soft blue eye he look'd upon the waves,
And talk'd of treacherous rocks, and seamen's graves.
There was much sweetness in his boyish smile,
And signs of feelings frank, that knew not guile.
The partial mother, of her darling proud,
Besought my friendship, and her own avow'd;
She praised her Rupert's person, spirit, ease,
How fond of study, yet how form'd to please.
In our discourse he often bore a part,
And talk'd, heaven bless him, of his feeling heart;
He spoke of pleasures souls like his enjoy,
And hated Lovelace like a virtuous boy;
He felt for Clementina's holy strife,
And was Sir Charles as large and true as life;
For Virtue's heroines was his soul distress'd;
True love and guileless honour fill'd his breast,
When, as the subjects drew the frequent sigh,
The tear stood trembling in his large blue eye,
And softly he exclaim'd, "Sweet, sweetest sympathy!"
When thus I heard the handsome stripling speak,
I smiled assent, and thought to pat his cheek;
But when I saw the feelings blushing there,
Signs of emotions strong, they said—forbear!
The youth would speak of his intent to live
On that estate which heaven was pleased to give—
There with the partner of his joys to dwell,
And nurse the virtues that he loved so well;
The humble good of happy swains to share,
And from the cottage drive distress and care;
To the dear infants make some pleasures known,
And teach, he gravely said, the virtues to his own.

He loved to read in verse, and verse-like prose,
The softest tales of love-inflicted woes;
When, looking fondly, he would smile and cry,
"Is there not bliss in sensibility?"
We walk'd together, and it seem'd not harm
In linking thought with thought, and arm with arm
Till the dear boy would talk too much of bliss,
And indistinctly murmur—"such as this."
When no maternal wish her heart beguiled,
The lady call'd her son "her darling child;"
When with some nearer view her speech began,
She changed her phrase, and said, "the good young man!"
And lost, when hinting of some future bride,
The woman's prudence in the mother's pride.
Still decent fear and conscious folly strove
With fond presumption and aspiring love;
But now too plain to me the strife appear'd,
And what he sought I knew, and what he fear'd:
The trembling hand and frequent sigh disclosed
The wish that prudence, care, and time opposed.
Was I not pleased, will you demand?—Amused
By boyish love, that woman's pride refused?
This I acknowledge, and from day to day
Resolved no longer at such game to play;
Yet I forbore, though to my purpose true,
And firmly fix'd to bid the youth adieu.
There was a moonlight eve, serenely cool,
When the vast ocean seem'd a mighty pool;
Save the small rippling waves that gently beat,
We scarcely heard them falling, at our feet.
His mother absent, absent every sound
And every sight that could the youth confound;
The arm, fast lock'd in mine, his fear betray'd,
And, when he spoke not, his designs convey'd;
He oft-times gasp'd for breath, he tried to speak,
And studying words, at last had words to seek.
Silent the boy, by silence more betray'd,
And fearing lest he should appear afraid,
He knelt abruptly, and his speech began—
"Pity the pangs of an unhappy man."
"Be sure," I answer'd, "and relieve them too—
But why that posture? What the woes to you?
To feel for others' sorrows is humane,
But too much feeling is our virtue's bane.
"Come, my dear Rupert! now your tale disclose,
That I may know the sufferer and his woes.
Know, there is pain that wilful man endures,
That our reproof and not our pity cures;

For though for such assumed distress we grieve,
Since they themselves as well as us deceive,
Yet we assist not."—The unhappy youth,
Unhappy then, beheld not all the truth.
"O! what is this?" exclaim'd the dubious boy;
"Words that confuse the being they destroy?
So have I read the gods to madness drive
The man condemn'd with adverse fate to strive.
O! make thy victim, though by misery, sure,
And let me know the pangs I must endure;
For, like the Grecian warrior, I can pray,
Falling, to perish in the face of day."
"Pretty, my Rupert; and it proves the use
Of all that learning which the schools produce.
But come, your arm—no trembling, but attend
To sober truth, and a maternal friend.
"You ask for pity?"—"O! indeed I do."
"Well then, you have it, and assistance too:
Suppose us married!"—"O! the heavenly thought!"
"Nay—nay, my friend, be you by wisdom taught;
For wisdom tells you, love would soon subside,
Fall, and make room for penitence and pride;
Then would you meet the public eye, and blame
Your private taste, and be o'erwhelm'd with shame:
How must it then your bosom's peace destroy
To hear it said, 'The mother and her boy!'
And then to show the sneering world it lies,
You would assume the man, and tyrannize;
Ev'n Time, Care's general soother, would augment
Your self-reproaching, growing discontent.
"Add twenty years to my precarious life,
And lo! your aged, feeble, wailing wife;
Displeased, displeasing, discontented, blamed;
Both, and with cause, ashaming and ashamed.
When I shall bend beneath a press of time,
Thou wilt be all erect in manhood's prime;
Then wilt thou fly to younger minds t' assuage
Thy bosom's pain, and I in jealous age
Shall move contempt, if still; if active, rage;
And, though in anguish all my days are past,
Yet far beyond thy wishes they may last—
May last till thou, thy better prospects fled,
Shall have no comfort when thy wife is dead.
"Then thou in turn, though none will call thee old,
[Wilt] feel thy spirit fled, thy bosom cold;
No strong or eager wish to make the will,
Life will appear to stagnate and be still,
As now with me it slumbers: O! rejoice

That I attend not to that pleading voice;
So will new hopes this troubled dream succeed,
And one will gladly hear my Rupert plead."
Ask you, while thus I could the youth deny
Was I unmoved?—Inexorable I,
Fix'd and determined; thrice he made his prayer,
With looks of sadness first, and then despair;
Thrice doom'd to bear refusal, not exempt,
At the last effort, from a slight contempt.
"Did his distress, his pains, your joy excite?—"
No; but I fear'd his perseverance might.
Was there no danger in the moon's soft rays,
To hear the handsome stripling's earnest praise?
Was there no fear that while my words reproved
The eager youth, I might myself be moved?
Not for his sake alone I cried "persist
No more," and with a frown the cause dismiss'd.
Seek you th' event?—I scarcely need reply:
Love, unreturn'd, will languish, pine, and die.
We lived awhile in friendship; and with joy
I saw depart in peace the amorous boy.
We met some ten years after, and he then
Was married, and as cool as married men;
He talk'd of war and taxes, trade and farms,
And thought no more of me, or of my charms.
We spoke; and when, alluding to the past,
Something of meaning in my look I cast,
He, who could never thought or wish disguise,
Look'd in my face with trouble and surprise.
To kill reserve, I seized his arm, and cried,
"Know me, my lord!" when laughing, he replied,
Wonder'd again, and look'd upon my face,
And seem'd unwilling marks of time to trace;
But soon I brought him fairly to confess,
That boys in love judge ill of happiness.
Love had his day—to graver subjects led,
My will is govern'd, and my mind is fed;
And to more vacant bosoms I resign
The hopes and fears that once affected mine.

George Crabbe – A Short Biography

George Crabbe was born on December 24th, 1754 in Aldeburgh, Suffolk, and was the eldest of six
children fathered by George Crabbe Sr.

Crabbe was sent to school at a very young age and soon developed an avid and precocious interest in books. His father would often read passages from Milton and various 18th-century poets to him.

The family also subscribed to a country magazine called Martin's Philosophical Magazine. The Poet's Corner section was always given to Crabbe.

His father supported his son's interest in literature although obviously at that time thought his career would be in other areas.

Crabbe was sent first to a boarding-school at Bungay near his home, and a few years later to a more important school at Stowmarket, where he learnt mathematics and Latin, and a familiarity with the Latin classics. His early reading included the works of William Shakespeare, Alexander Pope, Abraham Cowley, Sir Walter Raleigh and Edmund Spenser.

Medicine had now been settled on as his future career and, after three years at Stowmarket, in 1768, he was apprenticed to a local doctor at Wickhambrook, near Bury St Edmunds. The doctor also kept a small farm, and Crabbe eventually spent more time doing farm labour and errands than medical work.

In 1771 he changed masters and moved to Woodbridge, here he joined a small club of young men who met at an inn for evening discussions. It was here that he also met his future wife, Sarah Elmy. Crabbe called her "Mira", and now, writing poetry, he would often refer to her as such in his poems.

In 1772, a lady's magazine offered a prize for the best poem on 'hope'. Crabbe entered and won. The magazine then printed other short pieces of his during the year.

His first major work, a satirical poem of nearly 400 lines called Inebriety, was self-published in 1775. Crabbe later said of the poem, which received little attention at the time, "Pray let not this be seen... there is very little of it that I'm not heartily ashamed of."

By this time he had completed his medical training and had returned to Aldeburgh. Low finances meant his intention to go to London to study at a hospital was abandoned and a job was taken as a warehouseman.

The following year, 1777, Crabbe did travel to London to practice medicine, but returned home with financial woes after a year. He continued to practice as a surgeon after returning, but with limited surgical skills, he received only the poorest of patients, together with small and undependable fees. This hurt his chances of an early marriage, but Sarah stayed devoted to him.

He moved to London again in April 1780, to see if he could make it as a poet, or, if that failed, as a doctor. By the end of May he had been forced to pawn his surgical instruments. But he had composed a number of works but, sadly, all failed to be published. He now wrote several letters seeking patronage, but these were also refused.

Crabbe was able to publish a poem at this time entitled The Candidate, but it was badly received by critics.

He continued to rack up debts, and was pressed by his creditors. In early 1781 he wrote a letter to Edmund Burke asking for help, in which he included samples of his poetry. Burke was swayed by

Crabbe's letter and by meeting with him, giving him money to relieve his immediate wants, and assuring him that he would do all in his power to further Crabbe's literary career.

A short time later Burke told his friend Sir Joshua Reynolds that Crabbe had "the mind and feelings of a gentleman." Burke admitted Crabbe to his family circle at Beaconsfield. The time he spent with Burke and his family exposed him to further knowledge and ideas as well as new and valuable friends including Samuel Johnson. He completed his unfinished poems and revised others with the help of Burke's criticism. Burke helped him have his poem, The Library, published anonymously in June 1781, it was greeted with modest praise by critics, and some public appreciation.

Burke realised that Crabbe was more suited to be a clergyman than a surgeon. On his recommendation he was ordained to the curacy and then returned to Aldeburgh. His fellow townsmen resented his rise in social class. Burke now manoeuvred for Crabbe to be made chaplain to the Duke of Rutland at Belvoir Castle in Leicestershire.

The Duke and Duchess, were kind and generous to him as were their friends who enjoyed his literary works. But his relationship with the others in the household was tense. With the publication in May 1783 of his poem The Village, Crabbe achieved popularity with both the public and critics. Samuel Johnson said of it in a letter to Reynolds "I have sent you back Mr. Crabbe's poem, which I read with great delight. It is original, vigorous, and elegant."

It was decided that, as Chaplain to a noble family, Crabbe was in need of a college degree, and his name was entered on the boards of Trinity College, Cambridge, and through various influences Crabbe obtained a degree without residence. This was 1783, but almost immediately he received an LL.B. degree from the Archbishop of Canterbury. This allowed Crabbe to be given two small livings in Dorsetshire, Frome St Quintin and Evershot.

On the strength of these preferments and a promise of future assistance from the Duke, Crabbe and Sarah Elmy were married in December 1783, in the parish church of Beccles.

In 1784 the Duke of Rutland became Lord Lieutenant of Ireland. It was agreed that Crabbe would not go to Ireland, though the two men parted as close friends. The newly-weds stayed on at Belvoir for another eighteen months before Crabbe accepted a vacant curacy in Stathern in Leicestershire, moving there in 1785. The couple had four children of which only two sons survived; George (1785) and John (1787).

In October 1787, at age 35, the Duke of Rutland died in Dublin, after a short illness. The Duchess, anxious to have their former chaplain close by, was able to get Crabbe the two livings of Muston, Leicestershire, and Allington, Lincolnshire, in exchange for his old livings. Crabbe brought his family to Muston in February 1789.

Crabbe was also a coleopterist and recorder of beetles, and is credited for discovering the first specimen of Calosoma sycophanta L. to be recorded from Suffolk. He published an essay, in 1790, on the Natural History of the Vale of Belvoir. It includes over 70 species of local coleopterans.

In 1792, through the death of one of Sarah's relations and her older sister, the Crabbe family came into possession of an estate in Parham, which, at a stroke, removed all of their financial worries. Crabbe soon moved his family to the inheritance.

Crabbe's life at Parham was not happy. The former owner of the estate had been popular for his hospitality, while Crabbe's lifestyle was much more private. His solace here was the company of his friend Dudley Long North and his fellow Whigs who lived nearby.

After four years at Parham, the Crabbes moved to a home in Great Glemham, Suffolk, placed at his disposal by Dudley North.

In 1796 their third son, Edmund, died at the age of six. The death shredded Sarah's mental health and she never recovered. Crabbe, a devoted husband, tended her until her death many years later.

During his time at Glemham, Crabbe composed several novels, none of which were published. After Glemham, Crabbe moved to the village of Rendham in Suffolk, where he stayed until 1805. His poem The Parish Register was all but completed whilst here, and The Borough was also begun.

In September 1807, Crabbe published a new volume of poems which included The Library, The Newspaper, The Village and The Parish Register, to which were added Sir Eustace Grey and The Hall of Justice. It has been decades since his last publication but now, with this, he was seen as an important poet. Four editions were issued in 18 months. The reviews were unanimous in approval, headed by Francis Jeffrey in the critically important Edinburgh Review.

In 1809 Crabbe sent a copy of his poems to Walter Scott, who, in reply told Crabbe "how for more than twenty years he had desired the pleasure of a personal introduction to him, and how, as a lad of eighteen, he had met with selections from The Village and The Library in The Annual Register." This exchange of letters led to a friendship that lasted for the rest of their lives.

The success of The Parish Register encouraged Crabbe to proceed with a far longer poem, which he had been working on for several years. The Borough was begun at Rendham in Suffolk in 1801, continued at Muston after his return in 1805, and finally completed during a long visit to Aldeburgh in the autumn of 1809. It was published in 1810. In spite of its defects, The Borough was an outright success and went through six editions in the next six years. (Benjamin Britten's opera Peter Grimes is based on The Borough).

The following three years were especially lonely for him. His two sons, George and John, and were now clergymen themselves, each holding a local curacy enabling them to live under the parental roof, but Sarah's health was very poor, and Crabbe had no-one to help him with her care for most of the time.

Crabbe's next volume of poetry, Tales was published in the summer of 1812. It received a warm welcome from the poet's admirers, and was again warmly reviewed by Jeffrey in the Edinburgh Review. It is now considered Crabbe's masterpiece.

In the summer of 1813, Sarah felt well enough to visit London again. Crabbe, Sarah and their two sons spent nearly three months there. Crabbe was able to visit Dudley North and some of his other old friends, and to visit and help the poor and distressed, remembering his own want and misery in the great city thirty years earlier. The family returned to Muston in September, and at October's end Sarah died at the age of 63. Within days of her death Crabbe fell seriously ill. He rallied, however, and returned to the duties of his parish.

In 1814, he became Rector of Trowbridge in Wiltshire, a position given to him by the new Duke of Rutland. He now remained at Trowbridge for the rest of his life.

His two sons followed him, as soon as their existing engagements allowed them to leave Leicestershire. The younger son, John, became his father's curate, and the elder, became curate at Pucklechurch, also nearby. Crabbe's reputation as a poet continued to grow in these years. This made him a welcome guest in many houses. Nearby was the poet William Lisle Bowles, who introduced Crabbe to the noble family at Bowood House, home of the Marquess of Lansdowne, who was always ready to welcome those distinguished in literature and the arts. It was at Bowood House that Crabbe first met the poet Samuel Rogers, who became a close friend and had an influence on Crabbe's poetry. In 1817, on the advice of Rogers, Crabbe stayed in London in the early summer to enjoy the literary society of the capital. Here he met Thomas Campbell, and through him and Rogers was introduced to his future publisher John Murray.

In June 1819, Crabbe published his collection Tales of the Hall.

Around 1820 Crabbe began suffering from frequent severe attacks of neuralgia, and this, together with his advancing years, made him less and less able to travel to London.

In the spring of 1822, Crabbe met Walter Scott for the first time in London, and promised to visit him in Scotland in the fall. He kept this promise during George IV's visit to Edinburgh.

Later in 1822, Crabbe was invited to spend Christmas at Belvoir Castle, but weather made the trip impossible. While at home, he continued to write a large amount of poetry (eventually leaving 21 manuscript volumes at his death).

Crabbe continued to visit at Hampstead throughout the 1820s, often meeting the writer Joanna Baillie and her sister Agnes.

In November 1832 he went to see his son George, at Pucklechurch. He was able to preach twice for his son, who congratulated him on the power of his voice, and other encouraging signs of strength. "I will venture a good sum, sir," he said, "that you will be assisting me ten years hence." "Ten weeks" was Crabbe's answer, and the prediction proved eerily accurate. Crabbe now returned to Trowbridge.

Early in January of the New Year he reported more drowsiness and increasing weakness. Later in the month he was laid low by a severe cold. Further complications arose, and it soon became apparent that he would not live much longer.

George Crabbe died on February 3rd, 1832, aged 77 at Trowbridge, Wiltshire with his two sons by his side.

George Crabbe – A Concise Bibliography

Sketch of Crabbe (1826)
Inebriety (1775)
The Candidate (1780)
The Library (1781)

The Village (1782)
The Newspaper (1785)
Poems (1807)
The Borough (1810)
Tales in Verse (1812)
Tales of the Hall (1819)
Posthumous Tales (1834)